# THE
# WHOLEFOOD
# COOKBOOK

### Pamela Westland

# THE WHOLEFOOD COOKBOOK

## Pamela Westland

TREASURE PRESS

First published in Great Britain in 1985 by
Octopus Books Limited

This edition published in 1987 by
Treasure Press
Michelin House
81 Fulham Road
London SW3 6RB

© 1985 Hennerwood Publications Limited

Reprinted 1988

ISBN 1 85051 216 7

Printed by Mandarin Offset in Hong Kong

The food that we eat day in and day out affects our health and well-being in every way. This message, obvious though it may seem, has taken a long time to get through to us. It is only in the last very few years that we have begun to give priority to the quality of the ingredients we use; choosing wholewheat flour and bread, for example, in place of the light-as-a-feather refined and very much processed white equivalent; brown rice with its delicious nutty flavour in place of the incomplete white grain, and exploring the exciting culinary possibilities offered by dried pulses, packed as they are with nutrients and dietary fibre.

Once you start looking into the range and extent of wholefoods on sale in shops and health foods shops, markets and supermarkets, you will find that they open up for you a whole new world of taste, texture, and that good old-fashioned term, 'goodness'.

Indeed, in a sense wholefoods themselves *are* old-fashioned. They might be a new and pleasant experience to many of us, but they were the only ingredients, the unadulterated products of the farms and cottage gardens, that our ancestors knew. That's why so many of the delicious wholefood recipes have a familiar and traditional ring – Jugged beef, Spiced fish cakes, Old-fashioned pease pudding, Greengage brandy snap cups, and Fennel rye bread among them.

Though we eschew many of the products of modern food technology – the incomplete grains, the highly processed foods and all those crammed with chemical additives and artificial colourings – we are fortunate to be able to take advantage of present-day worldwide transport systems and storage methods. Unlike our grandparents, we can pick up natural foods and exotic flavourings from faraway places and extend our culinary repertoire accordingly. Most significant of these foods in nutritional terms are soya beans and all the derived soya products which allow us to produce high-protein meals with little or no meat or fish content. Most delicious, perhaps, are the tropical fruits and vegetables available to us in great variety throughout the year.

## What is wholefood?

Before putting each food department, as it were, under the microscope, it is as well to define the term 'wholefood' clearly. At the simplest, it means natural ingredients, grown or raised under natural conditions, with nothing added or removed.

Health food shops sell 'organically grown' fresh and dried fruit and vegetables which carry the assurance that they have been grown without the aid of chemical fertilizers, pesticides or fungicides, in soil enriched only with natural waste products such as humus and compost. Whether you decide to 'go the whole hog' and insist on produce of this kind – inevitably a little more expensive because of the comparatively small acreage grown and the lower yields achieved – is a matter of personal choice.

Along with fresh fruit and vegetables, whole grains and all the whole-cereal products (such as wholewheat, rye and barley flours and wholewheat and buckwheat pastas), nuts, seeds and pulses are the staples of a wholefood regime, given infinite variety with fresh herbs and dried spices.

Perhaps because wholefood menus make such imaginative and extensive use of these and other plant foods of all kinds, many people mistakenly think that a wholefood diet is necessarily a vegetarian one. This is certainly not the case – as our chapters devoted to meat, poultry, game and fish recipes show. There is also the question of how cattle and poultry are raised and whether you seek out free-range eggs and meat from animals fed naturally.

Just as meat has its place in wholefood cooking, it goes without saying that natural dairy products 'qualify' too. Whole, unskimmed milk, soft and hard cheeses, and butter are all legitimate wholefoods. But the recipes in this book impose slightly stricter limitations, and quantities of these foods high in animal fats and cholesterol are pared down. Where possible without too much sacrifice of flavour or texture, skimmed milk, vegetable margarine, low-fat yogurt and certain unrefined vegetable oils are substituted.

Perhaps the most confusing issue of all surrounds the matter of sweeteners. Refined white sugars and refined sugar coloured brown with caramel (often confused with natural raw sugars) obviously have no part in wholefood cookery. Natural raw sugars, and molasses, which retain minerals and trace elements, are, in that sense, wholefoods. One tongue-in-cheek argument against honey is that is *is* a refined product – by bees! As all these sweeteners are high in calories – and what dieticians refer to as fast-acting 'empty' calories at that – it is best wherever possible to use dried fruits for sweetening. They have concentrated fruit sugars, are very high in fibre, and can even look fabulous!

## Vegetables

If wholefoods and healthy foods were chosen on appearance alone, fresh vegetables would have few rivals: perhaps only fresh fruits would pip them at the post for sheer appetite appeal.

Cash in on this great plus factor and serve vegetables fresh whenever possible. Not only because they have such eye appeal, but because this is when they are at their most nutritious.

All vegetables are high in vitamins, either singly or in various combinations, and contain significant amounts of minerals, mainly calcium and potassium. Carrots – in common with other orange and red vegetables such as pumpkin, red peppers and tomatoes – are a strong source of vitamin A (carotene). Broccoli and spinach have vitamins A, B1 (thiamine), B2 (riboflavin) and C in abundance, and both cauliflower and potatoes are high in vitamins B1 and C. Mushrooms, green peas, spinach and watercress are good sources of iron.

Sadly, vitamins are soluble in water and dissipate even on exposure to heat, light and air. So for this reason it is best – without actually going to the lengths of munching on raw potato sticks – to serve vegetables raw in salads and as crudités with dips, pastes and dressings.

Even though as much as 40 per cent of vitamins B1 and B2 and up to 60 per cent of vitamin C may be lost in the cooking process, you cannot expect to consign family and friends to a diet of raw Brussels sprouts and garden peas (though I do have a friend whose favourite June breakfast is a plate of fat peapods and strawberries!). What is important is to prepare, cook and serve vegetables with as little time-lag as possible: as near as you can get to serving them 'straight from the garden'. In practical terms this means, at best, growing your own, or shopping about every other day from the local market stall, shop or store which has the fastest turnover.

Cook vegetables for the shortest time you can get away with – it's probably best to wean the family away from very tender vegetables in gradual stages, otherwise they might be tempted to send them back to the kitchen! Use the minimum amount of water when boiling – or rather simmering – vegetables, for fast-boiling releases even more vitamins. Steaming them over lightly salted water or, better still, stock, is preferable.

Never peel vegetables unless you really have to, perhaps if the skins are damaged or discoloured – as so many of the nutrients are just beneath the skin. Baked jacket potatoes illustrate how good they can be; small whole potatoes simmered or steamed in their skins are almost as good. Scrubbing all root vegetables with a stiff brush is a lot easier and quicker than peeling: so the method has time and motion study on its side, too!

## Pulses

Pulses are a very special type of vegetable, the dried seeds of leguminous plants, which is to say, all peas and beans. In this dried state they can be safely stored in a lidded container for at least a year – a great advantage in former times – though the longer the interval since harvest the longer they will take to cook. For this reason, cooking times in recipes can only be approximate.

All pulses have a high nutritional value, containing vitamins of the B group, proteins and calcium, iron and potassium in significant amounts. If they are combined in the same course with any grain or dairy product, then together they will provide all the amino acids the body needs – just as first-class proteins such as meat and fish do.

With the exception of lentils, all dried pulses need to be pre-soaked, to rehydrate them, before cooking, either in cold water overnight or, once they have been brought to the boil from cold, for 1 hour. Never add salt until the pulses are almost cooked – it is almost impossible to soften them – but cook them with all the flavouring vegetables (herbs, onions, garlic, celery and carrots) and spices you like.

The word of warning on page 63 bears repetition: **always fast-boil kidney beans for (to be safe) 15-20 minutes to get rid of harmful toxins.** Then and only then may they be added to stews, casseroles and soups.

Pulses come in all shapes and sizes, from the large milky white butter beans, so good with boiled bacon, to the small pink speckled pinto or Mexican beans; tiny bright green mung beans – the fertile seed of Chinese bean sprouts – and jet black kidney beans, the heart of African soul food; the elegant pale green flageolets, superb with garlicky lamb, and deep red kidney beans, the vehicle for red-hot chilli seasoning. Their uses – in soups, salads, dips, stews, casseroles, pasties and pies – is just as versatile. Good thing they're so good for you!

## Grains

Named after the Roman goddess of the harvest, Ceres, cereals or grains are the edible seeds of plants bred from wild grasses. They include wheat – especially important because it is the only one to produce flour with good rising properties – rice, corn, barley, oats, rye, millet and buckwheat.

In their natural state, stripped only of the inedible outer husk, grains are highly nutritious. In the refined or processed form, as white flour, white rice and pearl barley, they have been stripped of the germ, which contains vitamins of the B group, vitamin E, calcium, potassium, iron, copper, magnesium and fat, and the bran, packed with dietary fibre. Some sacrifice, in health food terms!

On the subject of terms, the very words used to describe the various types of flour and bread set a trap for the unwary. Wholewheat, wholemeal and whole grain are synonymous, and mean just what they say. The flour has been milled from the whole grain, and includes the germ and the bran. 'Wheatmeal' implies that a percentage of the germ and bran have been removed; exactly what percentage is often indicated in an accompanying figure. For example, 81 per cent and 85 per cent wheatmeal flour have had 19 per cent and 15 per cent respectively extracted. Since the term wheatmeal is so vague it can be – and is – applied to 'brown' flour. And this, like 'brown' sugar, can be nothing more than the refined (incomplete) white product, coloured.

By switching to wholewheat flour for all baking – not only bread, but pastry, biscuits and cakes – to wholewheat pasta made with the whole durum (hard) wheat flour and to brown rice, you are well on the way to a healthy and wholefood diet. Brown rice does take longer to cook than white (45 minutes as against 10-12 minutes) so when time is of the essence, opt for pasta. Wholewheat pasta, so superb with simple and quick vegetable sauces, is cooked to perfection in 10-12 minutes.

Each grain brings its own characteristic flavour to a dish, and recipes follow to fire your imagination to turn those staple foods into satisfying and homely fare – a casserole of vegetable and oats, a chicken and mushroom risotto using wheat groats instead of rice, croquettes of vegetables with cracked wheat (burghul) all prove the point deliciously.

Don't neglect these 'other' whole grains when it comes to accompaniments for meat and vegetables. Soak them overnight if possible in cold water, rinse and drain them and cook them in boiling water for 1-1½ hours. Or if time presses, buy the cracked grains which can be cooked in 15 minutes or so.

## Dairy products

'A little of what you fancy does you good' must surely be true of all those deliciously wholesome foods from the dairy. For whole milk, whole milk products, butter, cheese and eggs are good sources of vitamins A and D (much of the vitamin C is destroyed in pasteurizing), vitamins B1 (thiamine) and B2 (riboflavin), proteins and minerals – calcium, potassium and phosphorus. That's on the plus side.

What makes so many people now switch to low-fat skimmed milk, polyunsaturated vegetable margarine, low-fat yogurt and cottage cheese is the high fat and cholesterol content of whole milk.

Yogurt, which has become such a popular instant snack or dessert, has many uses in the kitchen. You will find it gives a delicious sharpness to cheese sauces – on baked vegetables, for example – makes a dreamy topping for everything from desserts to soup and salads, and can be used in place of cream in fools, syllabubs and ices.

Yogurt tends to separate unattractively when it is heated in liquid sauces, as when it is stirred into a casserole. Prevent this by stabilizing the yogurt (see page 12).

## Fats and oils

Medical experts have at last drummed into us that a high saturated fat intake is a major factor in the incidence of heart disease, the greatest single cause of death in the Western world. And a recent report by the National Advisory Committee on Nutrition Education (NACNE for short) has made practical recommendations on how painlessly, so to speak, every family can reduce the amount of fat it consumes each day. There are three groups.

Saturated fats, the ones which set solid at room

temperature, are mainly of animal origin (though coconuts have them in abundance too) and are the worst offenders. They are present in all 'whole' dairy products – milk, whole-milk yogurt, butter, cream and cheese – and in meat and meat products, not only in the obvious fat around a piece of steak or a lamb chop or the lumps of fat in salami, but the 'hidden' fat that marbles all red meats.

Polyunsaturated fats are liquid or soft at room temperature and are present as oil in fish, to a smaller extent in meats, and in plants. These plant oils are extracted for a number of domestic and industrial uses, most familiar perhaps as cooking and salad oils. Corn, sunflower, safflower and soya bean oils are high in polyunsaturates. It is this category of oils that is said to have the ability actually to lower the level of cholesterol – a fatty, wax-like substance – in the bloodstream.

The last category, the mono-unsaturated fats, seem to have little or no effect on the incidence of heart disease; to be neutral in effect. Olive oil is high in this type of fatty acids.

When it comes to assessing fat types and levels, margarines can cause a great deal of confusion. Some, the hard types sold in blocks, are made up of saturated (solid) fats; some soft margarines, sold in tubs, are high in polyunsaturates and some, known as low-fat spread, are actually a blend of hard margarines and water. Until you are familiar with the various properties of each brand, it pays to check the label.

At present far too much of our body energy (or calorie intake) is derived from fats – 38 per cent. The NACNE Report recommends that this should be cut to 34 per cent in five years' time and 30 per cent over a ten-year period, with the axe falling most heavily on saturated fats. As the Report also recommends an increase (to compensate) in carbohydrates, and in dietary fibre, in practical terms this means less red meats, less wholemilk dairy produce and more bread and cereals. A chicken instead of a joint of beef on Sunday, and a cottage cheese and date sandwich instead of a ham one.

### Fruit and dried fruit

Fruits must surely be the most delicious convenience food of all, and of course they are absolutely brimful of nourishment. All fruits are high in vitamin C, with blackcurrants at the top of the class. The yellow-coloured fruits especially – that's melons, apricots, peaches and gooseberries – are a good source of vitamin A (carotene) and dried fruits weigh heavily with thiamine (vitamin B1).

As it is with vegetables, so it is with fruits: cooking can destroy up to 50 per cent of the vitamin C and even 'open' freezing (without syrup) destroys about 20 per cent. So fresh fruit on the menu – for breakfast, lunch or supper – at least once a day makes sound nutritional sense.

Dried fruits are in effect the very essence of fresh fruits, being much more concentrated purveyors of the natural sugars, fructose, glucose and sucrose, and of dietary fibre. Fresh apricots, for example, consist of about 2 per cent fibre, dried apricots ten times as much.

Get into the habit of chopping up dried fruits to add to muesli; tossing a handful of dried vine fruits – raisins, sultanas and currants – into rice just before serving, and into salads and fruit salads; and using dried fruits increasingly to cut down on sugars and you will have captured the spirit of wholefood cookery.

### Salt

The way some people punish the salt shaker you'd think their lives depended on it. And they could well do. Recent researches have shown an excess intake of salt to be responsible for hypertension (and 40 per cent of us are prey to that), heart disease and brain haemorrhage.

Apparently we need only 500 milligrams a day of salt; or, more specifically, we need the 200 milligrams of sodium that it contains. But in the U.K. we have been treating our taste buds to very much more. Not all of this salt is shaken on to our plates at the table, of course. Processed foods of all kinds are laden with it.

You will find it easier to cut down on salt in cooking vegetables, rice, sauces and so on if you add herbs and spices. Fresh mint, marjoram or parsley with the vegetables, a touch of cinnamon or allspice with whole grains, a couple of bay leaves in the sauce, and who needs salt!

By preparing and serving fresh ingredients, in wholefood cooking we have the greatest possible measure of control over what we eat. And we can be confident that the food we serve is as natural, wholesome and delicious as can be. I hope the following recipes prove the point.

# SOUPS, STARTERS & SNACKS

There's a very fine line drawn these days between snacks, light lunch or supper dishes, starters and appetizers to serve with drinks. In this chapter we bring together ideas to suit all those occasions.

Fruit is high on the wholefood list of light and lovely ways to start a meal; the fish, egg and cheese dishes make substantial snacks to serve with wholewheat toast, crisp, crunchy sticks of fresh vegetables or a light salad; and whether they are warm and welcoming for the winter or chilled and refreshing for summer, soups are a versatile example of wholefood cooking.

A good stock gives them 'body' and brings out the full flavour of the other ingredients. You get the best results by making your own, using beef bones (roasted first on a tray in a moderate oven for 40-45 minutes), or a cooked or uncooked chicken carcass with chopped onions, carrots, celery and a bunch of herbs for flavouring. Cover with water, bring slowly to the boil, cover and simmer for 2-2½ hours. Strain, cool and store in the refrigerator or freezer. For a vegetable stock use well-washed vegetable peelings and trimmings with a little yeast extract to intensify the flavour.

## ALMOND SOUP

*Serves 4*

1 litre (1¾ pints) chicken stock
2 celery sticks, chopped
1 small onion, peeled and quartered
1 bouquet garni
2 bay leaves
1 mace blade
salt
freshly ground white pepper
225 g (8 oz) blanched almonds, ground
100 ml (3½ fl oz) sweet sherry
120 ml (4 fl oz) plain unsweetened yogurt
(see note below)
40 g (1½ fl oz) flaked almonds, toasted,
to garnish

*Preparation time: 15 minutes*
*Cooking time: 1 hour*

*If you use homemade yogurt, it will need to be stabilized before adding to the soup, otherwise it might separate. To do this, stir in 1 teaspoon flour and heat gently in a small pan, stirring constantly.*

1. Put the stock into a pan, add the celery, onion, bouquet garni, bay leaves and mace and season with salt and pepper.
2. Bring slowly to the boil, uncovered, and skim off any foam from the top. Cover the pan and simmer for about 25 minutes.
3. Strain the stock, discarding the flavourings, and return it to the pan.
4. Stir in the ground almonds, add the sherry, cover and simmer for 20 minutes. **F**
5. Stir in the yogurt and heat gently. Taste and adjust seasoning if necessary.
6. Scatter the soup with the toasted almonds. Serve hot.

**F** *Freeze for up to 3 months. Thaw at room temperature for 4-5 hours, then reheat and continue from step 5.*

## CHINESE BEAN-SPROUT SOUP

*Serves 4*

1 litre (1¾ pints) chicken stock
1 medium onion, peeled and quartered
2 carrots, scraped and quartered
4 spring onions, thinly sliced
225 g (8 oz) fresh bean-sprouts
salt
freshly ground black pepper
2 tablespoons soy sauce
2 tablespoons dry sherry
2 large radishes, sliced and quartered, to garnish

*Preparation time: 15 minutes*
*Cooking time: 30 minutes*

*1.* Put the stock in a pan with the onion and carrots, bring to the boil, cover and simmer for 20 minutes.

*2.* Strain the stock thoroughly and discard the all vegetables.

*3.* Return the stock to the pan, add the thinly sliced spring onions and bean-sprouts, and season with salt and pepper. Bring to the boil and simmer gently for 2-3 minutes.

*4.* Stir in the soy sauce and sherry, taste and adjust seasoning if necessary.

*5.* Serve the soup in individual dishes and garnish each one with radish slices.

# GINGERED PUMPKIN SOUP

*Serves 6*

1 kg (2¼ lb) slice of pumpkin, peeled, seeded and roughly chopped
1 piece fresh ginger, peeled
1 tablespoon sunflower oil
1 large onion, peeled and chopped
2 teaspoons ground ginger
1 teaspoon ground turmeric
2 large, ripe tomatoes, skinned and chopped
2 teaspoons soft light brown sugar
¼ teaspoon grated nutmeg
strip thinly-pared orange rind
600 ml (1 pint) chicken stock
salt
freshly ground black pepper
300 ml (½ pint) plain unsweetened yogurt
(stabilized if homemade, see page 12)
*To garnish:*
2 tablespoons chopped parsley
6 tablespoons pumpkin seeds

*Preparation time: 15 minutes*
*Cooking time: 40 minutes*

*1.* Put the pumpkin into a pan with the piece of ginger and cover it with water. Bring to the boil, cover the pan and simmer for 15 minutes, or until the pumpkin is tender. Drain thoroughly and remove the ginger.

*2.* Heat the oil in the pan and fry the onion over moderate heat for 2 minutes. Stir in the ground ginger and turmeric and cook for 1 minute.

*3.* Add the pumpkin, tomatoes, sugar, nutmeg, orange rind and stock and bring to the boil. Cover and simmer for 10 minutes. Cool slightly. Discard the orange rind. **F**

*4.* Liquidize the pumpkin mixture in a blender, then return the purée to the pan. Season with salt and pepper and stir in the yogurt. Heat gently. Taste and adjust seasoning if necessary.

*5.* Garnish the soup with the parsley and pumpkin seeds.

**F** *Freeze for up to 3 months. Thaw at room temperature for 4-5 hours, then reheat and continue from step 4.*

*From the left: Almond soup; Chinese bean-sprout soup; Gingered pumpkin soup.*

# CELERIAC AND ORANGE SOUP

*Serves 6*

1 celeriac, about 350 g (12 oz), peeled and roughly chopped
1 medium potato, peeled and roughly chopped
2 medium carrots, scraped and sliced
1 litre (1¾ pints) chicken stock
thinly pared rind of ½ orange
1 teaspoon grated orange rind
1 tablespoon orange juice
salt
freshly ground black pepper
6 tablespoons plain unsweetened yogurt
(stabilized if homemade, see page 12)

*Preparation time: 20 minutes*
*Cooking time: 45 minutes*

1. Put the celeriac, potato and carrots into a pan with the stock and bring to the boil. Cover the pan and simmer for 30 minutes, or until all the vegetables are soft.
2. Cut the orange rind into very thin matchstick strips. Place them in a saucepan with a little boiling water and boil for 10 minutes, then drain. Reserve for garnish.
3. Cool the vegetables and stock slightly, then liquidize in a blender.
4. Return the purée to the pan, add the grated orange rind and juice and season with salt and pepper. Bring back to the boil and simmer for 5 minutes. **F**
5. To serve, pour the soup into individual dishes or bowls, swirl 1 tablespoon yogurt on to each portion and garnish with strips of orange rind.

**F** *Freeze for up to 3 months. Thaw at room temperature for 4-5 hours, then reheat and continue from step 5.*

# CURRIED CAULIFLOWER SOUP

*Serves 4*

1 tablespoon sunflower oil
1 medium onion, peeled and sliced
2 teaspoons curry powder (or to taste)
1 small cauliflower, roughly chopped
900 ml (1½ pints) chicken stock
salt
freshly ground black pepper
4 tablespoons sunflower seeds, to garnish

*Preparation time: 15 minutes*
*Cooking time: 30 minutes*

1. Heat the oil in a large pan and fry the onion over moderate heat for 2 minutes. Stir in the curry powder and cook for 1 minute.

2. Add the cauliflower and stock, season with salt and pepper and bring to the boil. Cover the pan and simmer for 20 minutes.

3. Cool slightly, then liquidize the vegetables and stock in a blender. Ⓕ

4. Return the purée to the pan. Taste and adjust the seasoning if necessary and reheat.

5. Garnish the soup with the sunflower seeds.

**Variation:** *To add interesting texture to the soup, cut off a few very small cauliflower florets before blending and set them aside. Add them to the purée in the pan.*

Ⓕ *Freeze for up to 3 months. Thaw at room temperature for 4-5 hours, then reheat and garnish with sunflower seeds.*

# SWEETCORN SOUP

*Serves 6-8*

1.5 litres (2½ pints) chicken stock
1 medium onion, thinly sliced
1 medium leek, white part only, thinly sliced
2 medium potatoes, peeled and diced
salt
freshly ground black pepper
150 ml (¼ pint) milk or buttermilk
350 g (12 oz) sweetcorn kernels
175 g (6 oz) can baby sweetcorn heads (from Oriental grocers), (optional)
2 tablespoons chopped parsley

*Preparation time: 15 minutes*
*Cooking time: 30 minutes*

1. Put the stock into a large pan with the onion, leek and potatoes, season with salt and pepper and bring to the boil. Cover the pan and simmer for 20 minutes. Cool slightly, then liquidize in a blender. Ⓕ

2. Return the puree to the pan and stir in the milk. Add the corn kernels and heads, if using, and heat gently.

3. Taste and adjust the seasoning. Stir in the parsley. Serve hot.

Ⓕ *Freeze for up to 3 months. Thaw at room temperature for 3-4 hours, then continue from step 2.*

*From the left: Celeriac and orange soup; Curried cauliflower soup; Sweetcorn soup.*

1. Heat the oil in a large pan. Fry the onion and garlic over a moderate heat for 4-5 minutes, stirring once or twice. Add the carrots, celery and potato, pour on the stock and add the tomatoes. Add the bouquet garni and season with salt and pepper.
2. Bring to the boil, cover the pan and simmer for 30 minutes, stirring occasionally. **F**
3. Add the macaroni, beans and courgettes, return to the boil, cover and cook for a further 15 minutes.
4. Taste and adjust the seasoning if necessary. Discard the bouquet garni and stir in the parsley. Serve hot, with the cheese handed separately.

**F** *Freeze for up to 3 months. Thaw at room temperature for 4-5 hours, then reheat over a low heat and continue from Step 3.*

## WATERCRESS SOUP

*Serves 6*

25 g (1 oz) butter
1 medium onion, peeled and finely chopped
3 spring onions, sliced
3 bunches watercress, trimmed and chopped
25 g (1 oz) wholewheat flour
1 litre (1¾ pints) chicken stock
salt
freshly ground black pepper
150 ml (¼ pint) plain unsweetened yogurt
(stabilized if homemade, see page 12)
small sprigs of watercress, to garnish

*Preparation time: 15 minutes*
*Cooking time: 40 minutes*

1. Melt the butter in a large pan and fry the onion, spring onion and watercress over a low heat for 10 minutes, stirring frequently.
2. Increase the heat to moderate, and gradually pour on the stock, stirring constantly. Season with salt and pepper, bring to the boil and cover the pan.
3. Simmer for 15 minutes.
4. Cool slightly, then liquidize in a blender. **F**
5. Return the purée to the pan, stir in the yogurt, taste and adjust seasoning if necessary. Reheat gently.
6. Serve the soup hot, garnished with the watercress sprigs.

**F** *Freeze for up to 3 months. Thaw at room temperature for 3-4 hours, then continue from step 5.*

## PASTA MINESTRONE

*Serves 6-8*

1 tablespoon sunflower oil
1 large onion, peeled and chopped
1 garlic clove, peeled and chopped
2 medium carrots, scraped and thinly sliced
2 tender celery sticks, thinly sliced
1 large potato, peeled and diced
1.5 litres (2½ pints) beef stock
350 g (12 oz) tomatoes, peeled and sliced
1 bouquet garni
salt
freshly ground black pepper
100 g (4 oz) wholewheat short-cut macaroni
175 g (6 oz) dried flageolet or other beans, boiled until tender and drained
2 courgettes, cut into matchstick strips
3 tablespoons chopped parsley
grated Parmesan cheese, to serve

*Preparation time: 15 minutes*
*Cooking time: 1 hour*

# RED PEPPER SOUP

*Serves 4-6*

1 tablespoon sunflower oil
1 large onion, peeled and chopped
2 garlic cloves, peeled and finely chopped
2 tablespoons sherry
3 large red peppers, seeded, cored and cut into
strips
1 medium potato, peeled and diced
2 tablespoons tomato purée
2 large tomatoes, peeled and sliced
1 litre (1¾ pints) beef stock
1 bay leaf
1 bouquet garni
salt
freshly ground black pepper
*To garnish:*
2 tablespoons plain unsweetened yogurt
sprigs of parsley or chervil

*Preparation time: 15 minutes*
*Cooking time: 45 minutes*

1. Heat the oil in a large pan and fry the onion over moderate heat for 4-5 minutes, stirring once or twice. Add the garlic and the sherry and stir well.
2. Stir in the peppers, potato, tomato purée and tomatoes and pour on the hot stock. Add the bay leaf and bouquet garni and season with salt and pepper. Stir well.
3. Bring to the boil, cover the pan and simmer for 30 minutes.
4. With a slotted spoon, remove 2 spoonfuls of peppers and set aside.
5. Discard the bay leaf and bouquet garni and liquidize the soup in a blender. **F**
6. Return the soup to the pan, stir in the peppers, taste and adjust seasoning and heat gently.
7. Garnish the soup with swirls of yogurt and sprigs of chervil or parsley. Serve hot.

**F** *Freeze for up to 3 months. Thaw at room temperature for 4-5 hours, then continue from Step 6.*

*Left, from the top: Pasta minestrone; Watercress soup.*
*Below: Red pepper soup.*

# APRICOT SESAME SOUP

*Serves 6*

225 g (8 oz) dried apricots, soaked overnight
2 medium carrots, scraped and sliced
1 medium onion, peeled and sliced
1 cinnamon stick
450 ml (¾ pint) chicken stock
2 teaspoons lemon juice
salt
freshly ground black pepper
150 ml (¼ pint) plain unsweetened yogurt
1 tablespoon clear honey (optional)
2 tablespoons sesame seeds, to garnish

*Preparation time: 15 minutes, plus overnight soaking*
*Cooking time: 1 hour 10 minutes*

1. Drain the apricots and measure 600 ml (1 pint) of the soaking water. Make the liquid up to that measure if necessary.
2. Put the apricots, liquid, carrots, onion, cinnamon, stock and lemon juice into a large pan and season with salt and pepper.
3. Bring to the boil, cover the pan and simmer for 1 hour. Remove the cinnamon stick. Skim off any fat that has risen to the surface. Allow the soup to cool, then liquidize in a blender. **F**
4. Beat in the yogurt. Taste and adjust seasoning if necessary. Chill the soup and serve it with a little honey drizzled over and garnished with the sesame seeds, in chilled bowls.

**Variation:** *You can also serve the soup hot, accompanied by oat-cakes. Stir in the yogurt after blending the soup, then reheat it gently.*

**F** *Freeze for up to 3 months. Thaw at room temperature for 4-5 hours, then continue from step 4.*

From the left: Apricot sesame soup; Gazpacho; Mushroom dairy soup.

## GAZPACHO

*Serves 6-8*

450 g (1 lb) tomatoes, peeled and sliced
900 ml (1½ pints) chicken stock, all fat removed
½ cucumber, peeled and chopped
1 garlic clove, peeled and chopped
1 green pepper, seeded, cored and sliced
50 g (2 oz) wholemeal bread, crusts removed, diced
4 tablespoons sunflower oil
salt
freshly ground black pepper
2 tablespoons red wine vinegar

*To garnish:*
½ cucumber, finely diced
1 red pepper, seeded, cored and finely chopped
1 green pepper, seeded, cored and finely chopped
4 spring onions, thinly sliced
2 tablespoons finely snipped chives
8 green olives stuffed with pimentoes, thinly sliced
2 tablespoons chopped parsley

*Preparation time: 30 minutes, plus 1 hour chilling*

1. Liquidize all the main ingredients in batches in a blender. Taste and adjust the seasoning if necessary.
2. Cover the soup and chill in the refrigerator for at least 1 hour.
3. Stir all the garnish ingredients into the soup. Serve chilled, in chilled bowls.

## MUSHROOM DAIRY SOUP

*Serves 4*

450 g (1 lb) button mushrooms
600 ml (1 pint) chicken stock, all fat removed
1 medium onion, peeled and sliced
½ teaspoon ground coriander
salt
freshly ground black pepper
600 ml (1 pint) buttermilk
2 tablespoons chopped mint

*Preparation time: 15 minutes, plus chilling*
*Cooking time: 15 minutes*

1. Reserve a few of the best-shaped mushrooms for garnish. Chop the remainder.
2. Put the mushrooms in a pan with the stock, onion and coriander and season with salt and pepper. Bring to the boil and skim off any fat that rises to the surface. Cover and simmer for 10 minutes. Cool slightly.
3. Liquidize the vegetables and stock in a blender. Cool. Ⓕ
4. Beat in the buttermilk. Cover and chill.
5. Just before serving, stir in the mint. Thinly slice the reserved mushrooms and scatter them over the soup to garnish.

Ⓕ *Freeze for up to 3 months. Thaw at room temperature for 3-4 hours, then continue from step 4.*

# VEGETABLE VELVET

*Serves 6*

1 large aubergine, about 225 g (8 oz)
75 g (3 oz) herb and cream cheese
100 g (4 oz) low fat soft cheese
1 tablespoon lemon juice
1 tablespoon chopped chervil or parsley
salt
freshly ground black pepper
1 lemon, quartered, to serve

*Preparation time: 20 minutes*
*Cooking time: 45 minutes*
*Oven: 190°C, 375°F, Gas Mark 5*

*A blend of aubergine and creamy cheeses, this dish makes a delicious dip to serve as a first course or with drinks. It is also a good sandwich filling, especially with rye wholewheat bread. It is best made no more than a few hours in advance. Store in the refrigerator in a lidded container.*

1. Prick the skin of the aubergine with a fork and place it on a baking sheet.
2. Cook the aubergine in a preheated oven for 45 minutes, turning it once or twice.
3. Cut the aubergine in half lengthways and scoop out the flesh.
4. Liquidize the aubergine flesh in a blender with the cheeses and lemon juice. Stir in the herb and season with salt and pepper.
5. Pile the mixture into a serving bowl and garnish with the lemon wedges. If liked surround the dish with fresh vegetable sticks – crudités, see page 26 – on slices of warm wholemeal pitta bread.

*From the left: Vegetable velvet; Baked Brixham avocadoes.*
*Opposite: Melon kontiki.*

# BAKED BRIXHAM AVOCADOS

*Serves 4*

2 avocados, halved and stoned
2 teaspoons lemon juice
200 ml (7 fl oz) plain unsweetened yogurt
2 tablespoons tomato purée
225 g (8 oz) fresh or thawed frozen crab meat, flaked
2 tablespoons grated Parmesan cheese
1 shallot, peeled and finely chopped
salt
freshly ground black pepper
large pinch of cayenne
2 eggs, beaten

*Preparation time: 15 minutes*
*Cooking time: 30 minutes*
*Oven: 180°C, 350°F, Gas Mark 4*

1. Crunch up 4 pieces of foil in a baking dish and stand the halved avocadoes on them, making sure they are level. Brush the cut surfaces with lemon juice.
2. Beat together the plain unsweetened yogurt and tomato purée. Stir in the crab meat, cheese, shallot and the remaining lemon juice and season with salt and pepper and cayenne. Beat in the eggs.
3. Divide the filling between the avocado halves.
4. Pour water into the dish to come halfway up the avocado shells. Cook in a preheated oven for 25-30 minutes, until the filling is set. Serve at once.

# MELON KONTIKI

*Serves 4*

1 large cantaloup or honeydew melon,
quartered and seeded
2 tablespoons port
1 tablespoon ginger syrup
2 kiwi fruits, peeled and sliced into rounds
matchstick strips of crystallised
stem ginger, to decorate

*Preparation time: 15 minutes, plus about 30 minutes chilling*

1. With a long, sharp knife, cut the melon flesh away from the rind, but leave it in place.
2. Stir the port and ginger syrup together and pour over the melon slices. Cover and chill for at least 30 minutes.
3. Cut the melon flesh into 12 mm (½ inch) slices. Leaving each pointed-end slice intact, push alternate slices to left and right.
4. Arrange slices of kiwi fruit in a line down the centre of each melon slice. Decorate with strips of ginger and serve chilled.

# ELIZABETHAN EGGS

*Serves 4*

25 g (1 oz) butter
1 small onion, peeled and very finely chopped
450 g (1 lb) young sorrel leaves, stripped from stalks
1 tablespoon lemon juice
salt
freshly ground black pepper
6 hard-boiled eggs, shelled and halved

*Preparation time: 15 minutes*
*Cooking time: 15 minutes*

*Sorrel, a leafy herb with a lemony scent, was very popular in Elizabethan times. If it is unavailable, you can use young and tender spinach leaves instead.*

1. Melt the butter in a pan and fry the onion over low heat for 5 minutes, stirring occasionally.
2. Add the sorrel, mix well and add in the lemon juice. Season with salt and pepper. Simmer gently for 5 minutes, stirring frequently with a wooden spoon.
3. Chop 2 of the hard-boiled eggs, keeping the whites and yolks separate, and reserve.
4. Press the sorrel sauce through a sieve and gently reheat it.
5. Place the halved eggs, cut sides down, on a serving dish. Serve them with the sauce and garnish with pieces of the chopped egg. Serve at once, as a first course or a light meal, with wholewheat bread.

# TANGY SWEET AND SOUR SALAD

*Serves 6*

1 small curly endive
2 small grapefruit (pink variety, if possible), peeled and segmented
2 small avocados, stoned, peeled and sliced
225 g (8 oz) cottage cheese

# TOMATO MOUSSE

*Serves 4*

25 g (1 oz) butter
1 small onion, chopped
1 garlic clove, finely chopped
6 large, ripe tomatoes, skinned, seeded and chopped
50 g (2 oz) button mushrooms, chopped
2 tablespoons mint leaves
½ teaspoon caster sugar
salt
freshly ground black pepper
1 teaspoon lemon juice
few drops of Tabasco Sauce
2 tablespoons hot water
1 tablespoon powdered gelatine
150 ml (¼ pint) soured cream
½ cucumber, to garnish

*Preparation time: 20 minutes, plus setting*
*Cooking time: 20 minutes*

1. Melt the butter in a pan and fry the onion and garlic over low heat for 5 minutes, stirring occasionally.
2. Add the tomatoes and mushrooms and continue cooking for 10 minutes, stirring frequently.
3. Remove from the heat and stir in the mint, sugar, salt, pepper, lemon juice and the Tabasco Sauce.
4. Put the hot water in a cup, sprinkle the gelatine on top and stir over hot water until it has dissolved. Stir the gelatine into the tomato mixture.
5. Liquidize the mixture in a blender. Taste the purée and adjust seasoning if necessary. Cool.
6. Stir the soured cream into the purée. Pour into a serving dish, cover and chill in the refrigerator for 2-3 hours to set. **F**
7. Using a potato peeler, pare off the cucumber peel in long, thin strips. Thinly slice the cucumber. Arrange the overlapping slices of cucumber around the dish.

**F** *Freeze the mousse for up to 1 month. Thaw overnight in the refrigerator.*

4 tablespoons sultanas
1 teaspoon grapefruit rind, cut into julienne strips
50 g (2 oz) toasted sesame seeds
*Dressing:*
2 tablespoons lemon juice
1 tablespoon clear honey
6 tablespoons tomato juice
¼ teaspoon mustard powder
salt
freshly ground black pepper

*Preparation time: 15 minutes*

1. Arrange the largest endive leaves to cover a serving plate and make a 'nest' of the smallest ones in the centre.
2. Combine the dressing ingredients and toss the grapefruit and avocado in the dressing.
3. Arrange a ring of alternating grapefruit and avocado slices around the plate on top of the endive. Pour over any remaining dressing.
4. Mix the cheese with the sultanas and grapefruit rind, pile it in the centre and scatter with sesame seeds.

*From the left: Elizabethan eggs; Tangy sweet and sour salad; Tomato mousse.*

## GRILLED SHERRIED ORANGES

*Serves 4*

4 large oranges
4 tablespoons dry sherry
2 tablespoons orange liqueur
1 tablespoon clear honey
*To garnish:*
3 tablespoons water
2 tablespoons clear honey
16-20 white grapes, seeded

*Preparation time: 15 minutes*
*Cooking time: 10 minutes*

1. Halve the oranges. Cut out the segments and discard the pith. Reserve 4 half shells.
2. Heat the grill to medium. In a small bowl mix together the sherry, liqueur, honey and the orange segments and pour into a small heat-proof dish.
3. Heat the water and honey for the garnish in a small pan over moderate heat and poach the grapes for 5 minutes.
4. Grill the oranges for 5 minutes, until they are hot. Pour them into the reserved orange shells.
5. Garnish the oranges with the grapes and serve at once.

## GREEK-STYLE ONIONS

*Serves 6*

200 ml (7 fl oz) red wine
4 tablespoons red wine vinegar
3 tablespoons sunflower oil
3 tablespoons tomato purée
40 g (1½ oz) soft light brown sugar
450 ml (¾ pint) water
1 kg (2¼ lb) button or pickling onions, peeled
4 tender celery sticks, thinly sliced
100 g (4 oz) seedless raisins
salt
freshly ground black pepper
3 tablespoons chopped parsley

*Preparation time: 15 minutes*
*Cooking time: 45 minutes*

1. Put the wine, vinegar, oil, tomato purée, sugar and water into a pan and stir over low heat to dissolve the sugar.
2. Add the onions, celery and raisins, season with salt and pepper and bring to the boil over moderate heat, stirring occasionally.
3. Cover the pan and simmer gently for 35 minutes, or until the onions are tender. Taste the sauce and adjust the seasoning if necessary.
4. Stir in 2 tablespoons of the parsley, and garnish with the remainder. Serve hot, with plenty of crusty wholewheat bread.

## BAKED HERBY MUSHROOMS

*Serves 4*

16-20 medium mushrooms
2 tablespoons sunflower oil
1 small onion, peeled and finely chopped
2 garlic cloves, crushed
6 tablespoons fresh wholewheat breadcrumbs
¼ teaspoon grated nutmeg
3 tablespoons chopped parsley
8 tablespoons grated Gouda cheese
2 tablespoons plain unsweetened yogurt
1 egg, beaten
salt
freshly ground black pepper

*Preparation time: 15 minutes*
*Cooking time: 20 minutes*
*Oven: 180°C, 350°F, Gas Mark 4*

1. Cut the stalks from the mushrooms and trim and chop them finely.
2. Heat the oil in a frying pan and fry the onion, garlic and chopped stalks over moderate heat for 3-4 minutes, stirring frequently.
3. Turn the mixture into a bowl and stir in the breadcrumbs, nutmeg, parsley, 4 tablespoons of the cheese and the yogurt. Bind the mixture with the beaten egg and season with salt and pepper.
4. Place the mushrooms, stalk side up, on a greased baking tray. Divide the filling between them. Sprinkle on the remaining cheese.
5. Bake in a preheated oven for 15 minutes, or until bubbling. Serve hot with triangles of toast.

*Clockwise from top left: Greek-style onions; Baked herby mushrooms; Grilled sherried oranges.*

## CRUDITÉS WITH DIPS

*Offer a selection of crisp, colourful vegetable 'dip-sticks' and savoury dips as appetizers to serve with drinks, or as a light and crunchy starter or snack.*

*Choose fresh, seasonal vegetables, and be sure you buy the best possible quality. Prepare them so that they are evenly matched for size – carrot, cucumber, celery and green pepper strips of equal length and thickness, trimmed spring onions, sliced button mushrooms and cauliflower florets graded for size. You can prepare them a day in advance and store them, each type separately, in lidded containers in the refrigerator.*

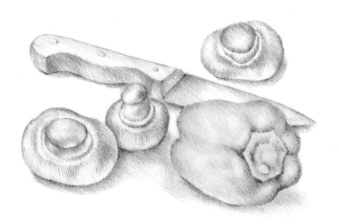

## LIPTAUER CHEESE DIP

*Serves 4-6*

25 g (1 oz) butter
175 g (6 oz) low fat soft cheese
1 teaspoon Dijon mustard
1 teaspoon anchovy paste
1 teaspoon paprika pepper, plus extra for garnish
1 tablespoon chopped gherkin
1 tablespoon chopped capers
1 teaspoon finely snipped chives, plus extra for garnish
freshly ground black pepper

*Preparation time: 15 minutes*

1. Beat the butter until it is soft. Beat in the cheese, mustard, anchovy and paprika and beat until the mixture is smooth. Stir in the gherkin, capers and chives and season with pepper.
2. Spoon the dip into a serving bowl and sprinkle on a little paprika and a few chopped chives to garnish.

# CELERY DIP

*Serves 4*

175 g (6 oz) low fat soft cheese
2 tablespoons plain unsweetened yogurt
3 tender celery sticks, finely chopped
2 tablespoons chopped celery leaves
1 teaspoon celery seeds
salt
freshly ground black pepper
chopped celery leaves, to garnish

*Preparation time: 15 minutes*

1. Beat the cheese and yogurt and stir in the chopped celery, leaves and seeds. Season with salt and pepper. **F**
2. Spoon the dip into a serving bowl and garnish with the celery leaves.

**F** *Freeze the dip for up to 2 months. Thaw at room temperature for 2 hours.*

*From the left: Crudités; Liptauer cheese dip; Celery dip; Butter bean dip.*

# BUTTER BEAN DIP

*Serves 4*

100 g (4 oz) dried butter beans, soaked overnight
and drained
4 tablespoons sunflower oil
2 garlic cloves, crushed
2 tablespoons cider vinegar
2 tablespoons chopped parsley
salt
freshly ground black pepper
chopped parsley, to garnish

*Preparation time: 15 minutes*
*Cooking time: 1 hour*

1. Cook the beans in boiling unsalted water for 1 hour, or until they are tender. Drain them, reserving the liquid, rinse in cold water and drain again.
2. Liquidize the beans in a blender with the oil, garlic, vinegar and 3 tablespoons of the reserved liquid.
3. Stir in the parsley and season with salt and pepper. Garnish with the chopped parsley.

## PRAWN PUFFS

*Serves 6*

300 ml (½ pint) water
50 g (2 oz) margarine
100 g (4 oz) wholewheat flour
1 teaspoon dried mixed herbs
pinch of salt
2 large eggs
*Filling:*
225 g (8 oz) low fat soft cheese
100 g (4 oz) shelled prawns, chopped
1 tablespoon chopped parsley
1 teaspoon lemon juice
pinch of cayenne
freshly ground black pepper

*Preparation time: 30 minutes*
*Cooking time: 30 minutes*
*Oven: 200° C, 400° F, Gas Mark 6*

1. In a small pan, heat the water and margarine to boiling point. Stir together the flour, herbs and salt. Tip the fat mixture at once on to the flour and stir vigorously. Beat in the eggs one at a time, beating continuously.
2. Using 2 dessertspoons to shape rounds of the mixture, place them well apart on a greased baking tray.
3. Bake in a preheated oven for 15-20 minutes, or until the buns are well risen and sound hollow when tapped.
4. Split the buns open to allow the steam to escape and leave them on a wire rack to cool. Store for up to 1 day in an airtight tin.
5. Beat the filling ingredients together. Fill the buns just before serving and accompany with a salad garnish.

*Clockwise from top left: Potted cheese; Hundreds and thousands pâté; Finnan cocottes; Prawn puffs.*

# POTTED CHEESE

*Serves 4-6*

50 g (2 oz) low fat cheese spread
175 g (6 oz) Wensleydale cheese, grated
40 g (1½ oz) Roquefort cheese, crumbled
4 tablespoons plain unsweetened yogurt
2 tablespoons medium sherry
freshly ground black pepper
1 tablespoon chopped parsley
bay leaves or parsley sprigs, to garnish
wholemeal bread slices

*Preparation time: 20 minutes*

1. Beat the low fat spread until it is soft. Beat in the cheeses and yogurt and then the sherry, a few drops at a time. Season with pepper and stir in the parsley.
2. Spoon the cheese into a serving bowl or individual dishes and level the top. Cover the dish and chill. F Garnish with the bay leaves or parsley sprigs.
3. Using biscuit cutters, cut the bread into hearts or other decorative shapes. Toast the shapes and serve with the potted cheese.

F *Freeze the potted cheese for up to 1 month. Thaw in the refrigerator for 3-4 hours.*

# HUNDREDS AND THOUSANDS PÂTÉ

*Serves 6-8*

225 g (8 oz) smoked cod's roe
225 g (8 oz) low fat soft cheese
2 tablespoons lemon juice
1 hard-boiled egg, finely chopped
1 tablespoon sunflower oil
freshly ground black pepper
8 tablespoons condensed consommé
1 tablespoon medium sherry
1 teaspoon powdered gelatine
*To garnish:*
chervil leaves
red and black lumpfish roe

*Preparation time: 30 minutes, plus setting*
*Cooking time: 3 minutes*

1. Put the cod's roe in a bowl and pour on boiling water to cover. Drain the roe, cool slightly and peel off the skin. Mash the roe to break it up.

2. Mix together the roe, cheese, lemon juice, chopped egg and sunflower oil and beat well. Taste and season the mixture with pepper, then spoon into a serving dish.
3. Heat the consommé with the sherry, stir in the gelatine and dissolve. Set aside to cool.
4. When the gelatine mixture is like unbeaten egg white, spoon it over the pâté. Cover and put in the refrigerator to set.
5. Garnish the pâté with the herbs and the red and black lumpfish roe arranged like bunches of grapes.

# FINNAN COCOTTES

*Serves 4*

225 g (8 oz) smoked haddock fillet
2 bay leaves
6 black peppercorns
225 g (8 oz) cottage cheese
3 spring onions, chopped
100 g (4 oz) button mushrooms, chopped
2 eggs, beaten
1 tablespoon lemon juice
salt
freshly ground black pepper
3 tablespoons fresh wholemeal breadcrumbs
1 tablespoon grated Parmesan cheese
1 teaspoon paprika
4 lemon slices, to garnish, (optional)

*Preparation time: 15 minutes*
*Cooking time: 45 minutes*
*Oven: 180°C, 350°F, Gas Mark 4*

1. Place the fish in a pan with the bay leaves, peppercorns and just enough water to cover. Bring to the boil and simmer for 5 minutes. Drain, cool and flake the fish, removing the skin and any bones.
2. Mix the fish with the cottage cheese, onion and mushrooms. Stir in the beaten eggs and lemon juice and season with salt and pepper.
3. Divide the mixture between 4 greased cocotte dishes and level the tops. Mix together the breadcrumbs, cheese and paprika and sprinkle on top of each dish.
4. Stand the dishes in a roasting pan with water to come half-way up the sides. Cook in a preheated oven for 35 minutes, or until the mixture is just firm.
5. Serve hot, garnished with lemon slices, if liked, and accompanied by hot toast.

# SPICED FISH CAKES

*Serves 4*

450 g (1 lb) coley fillet (or other white fish),
skinned
300 ml (½ pint) skimmed milk
1 bay leaf
25 g (1 oz) low fat spread
1 small onion, peeled and finely chopped
1 green pepper, seeded, cored and finely chopped
½ teaspoon chilli powder, or to taste
25 g (1 oz) wholewheat flour
salt
1 egg, beaten
4 tablespoons wholewheat breadcrumbs
50 g (2 oz) peanuts, crushed or finely chopped
1 tablespoon milk
2 tablespoons sunflower oil
celery stick, to garnish
*Sauce:*
3 spring onions, finely chopped
2 tablespoons chopped mint
1 teaspoon lemon juice
150 ml (¼ pint) Greek yogurt, chilled

*Preparation time: 25 minutes*
*Cooking time: 15 minutes*

1. Poach the fish in the milk with the bay leaf for 10 minutes, turning it once. Allow to cool slightly. Drain and chop the fish and reserve the milk.
2. Meanwhile, make the sauce. Beat the onion, mint and lemon juice into the yogurt. Chill in the refrigerator.
3. Melt the low fat spread and fry the onion and pepper over medium heat for 3 minutes, stirring once or twice. Stir in the chilli powder and cook for 1 minute. Stir in the flour. Pour on the reserved milk, stirring constantly until the sauce boils. Simmer for 3 minutes. Beat the sauce thoroughly.
4. Remove from the heat, beat in the fish and season with salt. Beat in half the egg. Leave the mixture to cool, then shape into 8 flat cakes. Mix together the breadcrumbs and the finely chopped peanuts.
5. Beat the remaining egg with the tablespoon of milk. Dip the fish cakes in the egg mixture and then in the breadcrumbs and peanuts, to coat. Heat the oil in a non-stick frying pan and fry the cakes for 3-4 minutes on each side.
6. Garnish with a celery stick and serve hot with the chilled sauce.

# GOLDEN SALAD

*Serves 4*

4 smoked mackerel fillets
2 large oranges, peeled and divided into segments
2 dessert apples, cored and thinly sliced
2 tender celery sticks, thinly sliced
2 tablespoons walnut halves
curly endive or lettuce leaves
4 thin orange slices, to garnish
*Dressing:*
1 teaspoon grated orange rind
3 tablespoons orange juice
2 tablespoons tomato juice
a large pinch cayenne
freshly ground black pepper
1 tablespoon clear honey
2 tablespoons finely snipped chives

*Preparation time: 20 minutes*

1. Skin the mackerel fillets and slice each one into 4 pieces.
2. Mix together the dressing ingredients.

3. Toss the oranges, apples, celery and walnuts in the dressing. Carefully stir in the mackerel.
4. Line a plate with salad leaves and spoon on the salad. Garnish with the orange slices.

## VINEYARD PARCELS

*Serves 6*

50 g (2 oz) dried apricots, soaked, drained and chopped
100 g (4 oz) cooked brown rice
100 g (4 oz) seedless raisins, chopped
50 g (2 oz) blanched almonds, chopped
1 cooking apple, peeled, cored and finely chopped
1 teaspoon grated orange rind
3 tablespoons orange juice
2 tablespoons clear honey
450 g (1 lb) bottle preserved vine leaves, well rinsed and drained
*Sauce:*
3 tablespoons orange juice
150ml (¼ pint) chicken stock

*Preparation time: 1 hour*
*Cooking time: 50 minutes*
*Oven: 180°C, 350°F, Gas Mark 4*

1. Mix together the apricots, rice, raisins, almonds, apple, orange rind and orange juice and the honey.
2. Spread 24 of the vine leaves out flat, stalk side towards you. Place a spoonful of the filling in the centre of each leaf. Roll up from the base, fold over the sides and wrap into a tight, neat parcel.
3. Cover a shallow baking dish with a layer of the remaining vine leaves and arrange the parcels in a single layer on top.
4. To make the sauce, mix together the orange juice and stock. Pour the sauce over the vine leaf parcels. Cover with any remaining leaves and cover the dish with foil. Cook in a pre-heated oven for 50 minutes. Remove the foil and serve hot.

*From the left: Spiced fish cakes; Vineyard parcels; Golden salad.*

# MEAT, POULTRY & GAME

Many people confuse wholefood cooking with a vegetarian diet and so, if they enjoy meat and fish dishes, they close their minds to the whole subject. This is a great pity as wholefood cooking embraces all natural and unadulterated ingredients, including high-protein foods such as meat and fish. However wholefood menus do tend to rely less on animal proteins, often to the extent of using a little meat in the Chinese way to complement and flavour grain and pasta, rather than as the main and predominant ingredient.

To prepare and cook meat in the most healthy way it is important to eliminate as much as possible of the visible and hidden fat. This means trimming off the fat you can see on chops, steak and so on, and frying cubed meat for casseroles in the very minimum of oil or – if you have a good-quality non-stick pan – none at all. If you dry-fry the meat in this way, you can discard the melted fat – and many of the calories – before proceeding with the dish. Remember, too, that poultry is better for you than red meat since its fat content is less, particularly if you remove the skin before cooking, and that free range birds and meat from animals who are not force fed or fattened with drugs have the best flavour.

# ROLLED BEEF

*Serves 4*

4 'minute' steaks, about 150 g (5 oz) each
15 g (½ oz) butter
2 tablespoons sunflower oil
1 tablespoon chopped parsley, to garnish
*Filling:*
225 g (8 oz) frozen spinach, thawed and well
drained
175 g (6 oz) low fat soft cheese
50 g (2 oz) button mushrooms, chopped
salt
freshly ground black pepper
pinch of grated nutmeg
*Sauce:*
1 tablespoon sunflower oil
1 medium onion, peeled and finely chopped
1 garlic clove, peeled and crushed
2 tablespoons tomato purée
450 g (1 lb) tomatoes, skinned and sliced
6 tablespoons chicken or beef stock
1 teaspoon dried oregano
½ teaspoon grated orange rind

*Preparation time: 30 minutes*
*Cooking time: 1¼ hours*
*Oven: 180°C, 350°F, Gas Mark 4*

*1.* To make the sauce, heat the oil in a small pan
and fry the onion over moderate heat for 3
minutes. Add the garlic and tomato purée, the
tomatoes, stock, oregano and orange rind and
season with salt and pepper. Bring to the boil,
uncovered, and simmer for 20 minutes.

*2.* To make the filling, beat the spinach and
cheese and stir in the mushrooms. Season with
salt, pepper and nutmeg.

*3.* Place each steak flat on the table. Spread with
the filling and roll up, Swiss-roll style. Tie each
roll in 2 places with string.

*4.* Heat the butter and oil in a flameproof
casserole and fry the beef rolls over moderate
heat for 5-6 minutes, turning them to brown
evenly.

*5.* Pour the sauce over the meat, cover and cook in
a preheated oven for 40-50 minutes.

*6.* Taste the sauce and adjust the seasoning if
necessary. Remove the strings. Serve the dish
garnished with the parsley.

*Clockwise from top left: Rolled beef; Jugged beef;*
*Rickshaw lamb.*

# RICKSHAW LAMB

*Serves 6*

1.4 kg (3 lb) loin of lamb, chined and layer of fat
and skin removed
225 g (8 oz) brown short-grain rice
freshly ground black pepper
*Marinade:*
1 tablespoon grated orange rind
3 tablespoons orange juice
1 large onion, peeled and sliced
2 tablespoons sunflower oil
2 tablespoons soy sauce
2 tablespoons clear honey
5 tablespoons dry cider
1 teaspoon ground cinnamon

*Preparation time: 30 minutes, plus marinating*
*Cooking time: 1¼ hours*
*Oven: 190°C, 375°F, Gas Mark 5*

## JUGGED BEEF

*Serves 4*

1 kg (2¼ lb) shin of beef, cut across the bone into
4×2.5 cm (1 inch) slices
3 tablespoons flour
salt
freshly ground black pepper
1 teaspoon grated orange rind
3 tablespoons sunflower oil
15 g (½ oz) butter
2 large onions, peeled and thinly sliced
350 g (12 oz) carrots, scraped and thinly sliced
2 garlic cloves, peeled and crushed
2 bay leaves
300 ml (½ pint) red wine

*Preparation time: 30 minutes*
*Cooking time: 2½ hours*
*Oven: 120°C, 250°F, Gas Mark ½*

*The dish is improved if it is made the day before serving. When it is completely cold, lift off the layer of fat on top.*

1. Toss the meat in the flour seasoned with the salt, pepper and orange rind.
2. Heat the oil and butter in a flameproof casserole. Fry the onions and carrots for 4-5 minutes over a moderate heat, stirring frequently, until they are just beginning to brown. Remove them with a slotted spoon and set them on one side.
3. Fry the meat gently until it is evenly browned on all sides.
4. Return the onions and carrots to the casserole, and add the garlic, bay leaves and wine. Stir well and bring to the boil.
5. Cover the casserole and cook in a preheated oven for 2 hours, or until the meat is tender. Taste and adjust the seasoning if necessary. Discard the bay leaves and skim off any fat that has risen to the surface. **F**

**F** *Freeze for up to 3 months. Thaw in the refrigerator overnight. Heat on top of the cooker until bubbling.*

1. Mix together all the marinade ingredients. Put the marinade into a strong polythene bag, add the lamb and tie the bag securely. Shake it to cover the meat on all sides. Place the bag on a plate and leave in the refrigerator for several hours or overnight. Turn the bag occasionally, if possible.
2. Drain the lamb, reserving the marinade. Put the lamb in a roasting pan, pour on 2 tablespoons of the marinade and 2 tablespoons of water and cover with foil. Bake in a preheated oven for 45 minutes. Remove the foil, baste the meat and cook for a further 30 minutes.
3. While the meat is cooking, put the rice in a pan. Measure the marinade, make it up to 600 ml (1 pint) with water and season with pepper. Bring to the boil, pour over the rice, cover the pan and simmer for 45 minutes, stirring occasionally.
4. Transfer the meat to a heated serving dish and surround it with the rice.

# VEGETABLE AND BARLEY HOTPOT

*Serves 4*

225 g (8 oz) pot barley, soaked
175 g (6 oz) streaky bacon, rind removed, cut in squares
2 large onions, peeled and chopped
1 garlic clove, peeled and crushed
6 celery sticks, thinly sliced
2 medium courgettes, thinly sliced
350 g (12 oz) carrots, scraped and thinly sliced
225 g (8 oz) button mushrooms, sliced
600 ml (1 pint) chicken stock
3 tablespoons chopped parsley
1 tablespoon tomato purée
salt
freshly ground black pepper
1 tablespoon soy sauce

*Preparation time: 20 minutes*
*Cooking time: 2¼ hours*
*Oven: 180°C, 350°F, Gas Mark 4*

1. Cook the barley in boiling water for 1 hour. Drain.
2. Fry the bacon in a flameproof casserole over moderate heat until it is crisp. Remove with a slotted spoon and set aside. Discard all but 2 tablespoons of fat in the casserole.
3. Fry the onions, garlic and celery for 2 minutes. Add the courgettes, carrots and mushrooms. Pour on the stock and stir in the barley and bacon. Stir in 2 tablespoons of the parsley, the tomato purée, salt, pepper and soy sauce and bring to the boil.
4. Cover the casserole and cook in a preheated oven for 1 hour. Taste and adjust the seasoning. Sprinkle on the remaining parsley and serve hot.

# COURGETTE LAYER PIE

*Serves 4*

4 tablespoons sunflower oil
450 g (1 lb) courgettes, sliced
225 g (8 oz) onions, peeled and thinly sliced
450 g (1 lb) minced steak
450 g (1 lb) tomatoes, peeled and sliced
½ teaspoon dried oregano
2 tablespoons chopped parsley
salt
freshly ground black pepper
75 g (3 oz) Wensleydale cheese, very thinly sliced
*Topping:*
300 ml (½ pint) plain unsweetened yogurt
2 eggs
pinch of grated nutmeg
50 g (2 oz) Wensleydale cheese, grated

*Preparation time: 30 minutes*
*Cooking time: 1¼ hours*
*Oven: 190°C, 375°F, Gas Mark 5*

1. Heat 3 tablespoons of the oil in a large frying pan and fry the courgettes for about 2 minutes on each side over moderately high heat, until they begin to brown. Remove the courgettes and set aside.
2. Heat the remaining oil and fry the onions over moderate heat for 3 minutes. Add the meat and fry gently for 5 minutes, stirring often.
3. Add the tomatoes, oregano and parsley and season with salt and pepper. Bring to the boil, cover the pan and simmer for 10 minutes, stirring occasionally.
4. In a shallow, greased baking dish, make layers of the meat sauce, courgettes and cheese slices.
5. To make the topping, beat together the yogurt, eggs, nutmeg and grated cheese and pour over the dish.
6. Bake in a preheated oven for 1 hour, until the topping is deep brown. ⓕ Serve hot.

ⓕ *Cool the dish, cover and freeze for up to 3 months. Reheat from frozen in the oven at 180°C, 350°F, Gas mark 4, for about 1¼ hours.*

# BEEF AND RAISIN MEATBALLS

*Serves 4*

450 g (1 lb) lean frying steak, finely minced
1 small onion, peeled and finely chopped
2 tablespoons seedless raisins, chopped
2 tablespoons walnuts, chopped
2 tablespoons chopped parsley
¼ teaspoon ground allspice
salt
freshly ground black pepper
1 egg, beaten
flour, for dusting
mint sprigs, to garnish
*Sauce:*
300 ml (½ pint) plain unsweetened yogurt
1 teaspoon lemon juice

*Preparation time: 20 minutes*
*Cooking time: 45 minutes*

1. Blend the meat in a blender or food processor until it is a smooth paste. Beat in the onion, raisins, walnuts, parsley and spice, season with salt and pepper and beat in just enough of the egg to bind the mixture to a firm paste.
2. Flour your hands and shape the mixture into rounds almost the size of golf balls. ⓕ
3. Place the meatballs in a single layer in a flameproof casserole. Pour on the yogurt and lemon juice and season with salt and pepper.
4. Cover the dish and simmer for 45 minutes. Serve garnished with the mint sprigs.

ⓕ *Open-freeze the meat balls, then transfer them to a rigid container and freeze for up to 1 month. Thaw in the refrigerator for 3-4 hours or at room temperature for 2-3 hours.*

*Clockwise from top left: Vegetable and barley hotpot; Beef and raisin meatballs; Courgette layer pie.*

# LAMB AND VEGETABLE COUSCOUS

*Serves 6*

450 g (1 lb) medium couscous
salt
2 tablespoons sunflower oil
1 kg (2¼ lb) lean leg of lamb, trimmed of excess fat
and cut into 5 cm (2 inch) cubes
12 button onions or shallots, peeled
1 teaspoon chilli powder
½ teaspoon ground coriander
1 tablespoon tomato purée
450 g (1 lb) tomatoes, peeled and sliced
about 300 ml (10 fl oz) beef stock (see page 11)
2 medium carrots, scraped and sliced
2 medium potatoes, peeled and diced
100 g (4 oz) frozen peas
100 g (4 oz) frozen green beans
2 tablespoons chopped coriander leaves, or
parsley, to garnish.

*Preparation time: 45 minutes*
*Cooking time: 2¼ hours*

*Couscous is produced from the semolina made from hard durum wheat. The semolina grains are moistened, coated with flour and 'expanded' to produce light and fluffy cereal grains. They are cooked by steaming for about 45-50 minutes, either over fast-boiling water or, as in this typically Algerian recipe, partly over water and partly – for added flavour – over a meat or fish stew.*

1. Rinse the couscous in a colander under cold, running water. Fork over the grains to break up any lumps. Fit a steaming pan or a colander lined with a double-thickness of scalded tea towel over a pan of fast-boiling water. Add the couscous a little at a time, forking it through all the while. Season with salt and steam, uncovered, for 30 minutes.

2. Turn the couscous into a large bowl and pour on 450 ml (¾ pint) cold water. Mix well with a fork and set aside.

3. Heat the oil in a large pan, or the base of the steamer, and fry the lamb over moderate heat, stirring it to brown evenly. Stir in the onions, chilli powder and coriander and cook for 1 minute. Stir in the tomato purée, tomatoes and stock and bring to the boil.

4. Cover the pan and simmer for 1 hour.

5. Add the carrots and potatoes, cover and continue simmering for 15 minutes.

6. Add the peas and beans. Place the steamer or the colander lined with a tea towel on the pan. Place the couscous grains in the top, cover with a lid or foil and continue cooking for 15 minutes. Fluff up the grains with a fork from time to time.

7. Spoon the meat and vegetables into the centre of a heated serving dish and arrange the couscous in a ring around the outside. Garnish with the chopped coriander.

*Below: Lamb and vegetable couscous.*
*Right: Lamb in pepper cases.*

# LAMB IN PEPPER CASES

*Serves 4*

4 large green and yellow peppers
salt
2 tablespoons sunflower oil
225 g (8 oz) minced lean lamb
1 medium onion, finely chopped
50 g (2 oz) mushrooms, finely chopped
freshly ground black pepper
40 g (1½ oz) wholewheat breadcrumbs
1 teaspoon grated lemon rind
1 teaspoon lemon juice
2 tablespoons chopped parsley
2 tablespoons chopped blanched almonds
4 tablespoons plain unsweetened yogurt

*Preparation time: 20 minutes*
*Cooking time: 1¼ hours*
*Oven: 190°C, 375°F, Gas Mark 5*

1. Cut the tops from the peppers and set them aside. Scoop out the core and seeds.
2. Blanch the peppers and the tops in boiling, salted water for 5 minutes. Drain well.
3. Heat the oil in a pan and fry the meat over a moderate heat for 4-5 minutes, stirring frequently. Remove it with a slotted spoon. Fry the onion and mushrooms for 3 minutes, stirring once or twice. Return the meat to the pan and simmer, uncovered, for 15 minutes, stirring often.
4. Remove from the heat, season with salt and pepper and stir in the breadcrumbs, lemon rind, lemon juice, parsley, almonds and yogurt. Mix well.
5. Stand the peppers upright in a baking dish that just fits them. Fill them with the meat mixture and replace the lids.
6. Pour 5 cm (2 inches) of water into the dish, cover with foil and bake in a preheated oven for 50 minutes. Remove the foil 15 minutes before the end. Serve the peppers hot, with simmered brown rice.

# CASSOULET

*Serves 8-10*

1.5 kg (3½ lb) oven-ready chicken
450 g (1 lb) dried white haricot beans, soaked
overnight and drained
2 bay leaves
2 large onions, peeled and sliced
2-3 garlic cloves, crushed
1 bouquet garni
2 medium carrots, scraped and thinly sliced
1 kg (2¼ lb) lean lamb, cut into fingers
4 celery sticks, thinly sliced
450 g (1 lb) tomatoes, skinned and sliced
3 tablespoons tomato purée
1 teaspoon whole grain mustard
salt
freshly ground black pepper
2 tablespoons chopped parsley
1 tablespoon chopped parsley, to garnish

*Preparation time: 45 minutes*
*Cooking time: 5 hours*
*Oven: 150°C, 300°F, Gas Mark 2*

1. Put the chicken and beans in a large pan with the bay leaves, 1 sliced onion, the garlic and the bouquet garni. Cover with water, bring to the boil, cover the pan and boil for 10 minutes. Lower the heat and simmer for 1 hour.
2. Drain the chicken and beans, reserving the stock. Cut the flesh from the bones. Discard the bouquet garni and bay leaves.
3. In a large casserole, make layers of the chicken, beans, remaining onion, carrots, lamb, celery and tomatoes. Mix together the tomato purée, mustard and 1 litre (1¾ pints) of the reserved stock, season with salt and pepper and stir in the parsley.
4. Pour the stock into the casserole and cook, uncovered, in a preheated oven for 3 hours. F
5. Add a little more hot stock, if necessary, with the parsley sprigs and return to the oven for 45 minutes.

F *This is a dish that freezes particularly well, and is good to have made in advance for an informal party. Freeze for up to 3 months. Thaw at room temperature for about 12 hours.*

*From the top: Cassoulet; Loin of lamb Victoria.*

# LOIN OF LAMB VICTORIA

*Serves 4*

15 g (½ oz) soft margarine
1 small onion, peeled and finely chopped
1 tablespoon chopped parsley
75 g (3 oz) wholewheat breadcrumbs
225 g (8 oz) dessert plums, stoned and chopped,
plus 2 for garnish
1 large cooking apple, peeled, cored and chopped
salt
freshly ground black pepper
½ teaspoon ground coriander
2 tablespoons orange juice
1 kg (2¼ lb) loin of lamb, boned
parsley sprigs, to garnish
*Sauce:*
1 tablespoon flour
300 ml (½ pint) chicken stock
2 tablespoons port
2 tablespoons redcurrant jelly

*Preparation time: 30 minutes*
*Cooking time: 1 hour 20 minutes*
*Oven: 190°C, 375°F, Gas Mark 5*

1. Melt the margarine in a pan and fry the onion over moderate heat for 3 minutes, stirring once or twice.
2. Remove the pan from the heat and stir in the parsley, breadcrumbs, plums and apple and season with salt, pepper and coriander. Stir in the orange juice and mix well. F
3. Spoon the filling into the cavity in the meat, roll it neatly and tie with string.
4. Place the meat in a roasting pan and cook in a preheated oven for 1-1¼ hours, until it is cooked to your liking.
5. Transfer the meat to a heated serving dish, cover with foil and keep warm. Pour off all but 1 tablespoon of the fat.
6. Over a moderate heat, stir in the flour. Pour on the stock, stirring constantly. Add the port and redcurrant jelly and season with salt and pepper. Bring to the boil and simmer for 3 minutes. Strain the sauce and serve it separately.
7. Stone and quarter the plums and use them with the parsley sprigs to garnish the meat.

F *You can freeze the stuffing separately in a rigid container for up to 1 month or freeze the uncooked, boned and rolled joint for up to 3 months. Thaw overnight in the refrigerator.*

# BOSPHORUS LAMB WITH FIGS

*Serves 4*

1.2-1.4 kg (2¾-3 lb) leg of lamb, boned
sliced, fresh figs, to garnish
*Filling:*
150 g (5 oz) dried figs, chopped
50 g (2 oz) fresh wholewheat breadcrumbs
1 small onion, peeled and finely chopped
1 teaspoon grated orange rind
3 tablespoons orange juice
¼ teaspoon ground cinnamon
salt
freshly ground black pepper

*Preparation time: 25 minutes*
*Cooking time: about 1½ hours*
*Oven: 190°C, 375°F, Gas Mark 5*

1. Mix together all the ingredients for the filling.
2. Press the filling into the cavity in the meat, close it to make a neat shape and tie with string.
3. Place the meat on a wire rack in a roasting pan and cook in a preheated oven for 1½ hours, or until the meat is cooked to your liking.
4. Remove the strings, transfer the meat to a heated serving dish and garnish the dish with the sliced figs.

# GALWAY STEW

*Serves 4*

1 kg (2¼ lb) potatoes, peeled and sliced
1.5 kg (3½ lb) best end of neck of lamb chops, trimmed of excess fat
450 g (1 lb) onions, peeled and sliced
4 leeks, white part only, sliced
salt
freshly ground black pepper
2 tablespoons chopped parsley
1 teaspoon dried thyme
450 ml (¾ pint) chicken stock
1 tablespoon tomato purée
1 tablespoon chopped parsley, to garnish

*Preparation time: 20 minutes*
*Cooking time: 3 hours*
*Oven: 140°C, 275°F, Gas Mark 1*

1. In a large casserole, make layers of potatoes, lamb chops, onions and leeks, seasoning with salt and pepper and sprinkling parsley and thyme between each layer. Begin and end with a layer of potatoes, overlapping the potato slices in neat rings to form the 'crust'.
2. Mix together the stock and tomato purée and pour into the casserole.
3. Cover the dish with a layer of foil and the lid. Cook in a preheated oven for 2 hours. Remove the foil and lid and add a little more stock or water if needed.
4. Return the dish to the oven, uncovered, for a further 1 hour, to brown the potatoes. Sprinkle with chopped parsley and serve with a green vegetable and plenty of wholewheat bread.

*Left, from the top: Galway stew; Bosphorus lamb with figs.*
*Right, from the top: Mushrooms and liver provençal; Stir-fried pork and cashews.*

1. Toss the liver slices in the flour seasoned with the salt, pepper and marjoram.
2. Melt the margarine and oil in a frying pan and fry the liver for 2 minutes on each side over a moderate heat. Remove the liver.
3. Fry the garlic, onion, peppers and mushrooms for 2 minutes, stirring. Add the tomatoes, sugar and vinegar. Stir well and return the liver to the frying pan.
4. Cover the pan and simmer for 10-15 minutes.
5. While the liver is cooking, cook the noodles in boiling, salted water for 10 minutes, or according to packet instructions, until tender.

# STIR-FRIED PORK AND CASHEWS

*Serves 4*

3 tablespoons sunflower oil
450 g (1 lb) fillet of pork (tenderloin), trimmed and cut into 5 mm (¼ inch) matchstick strips
1 garlic clove, peeled and crushed
1 slice fresh ginger, peeled and finely chopped
6 spring onions, sliced
100 g (4 oz) cashew nuts
1 red pepper, cored, seeded and thinly sliced
100 g (4 oz) bean-sprouts
*Sauce:*
1 tablespoon cornflour
5 tablespoons chicken stock
5 tablespoons dry sherry
2 tablespoons orange juice
1 tablespoon soy sauce
freshly ground black pepper

*Preparation time: 20 minutes*
*Cooking time: 10 minutes*

1. To make the sauce, put the cornflour into a bowl, pour on the chicken stock and stir it to a paste. Stir in the sherry, orange juice and soy sauce and season with pepper.
2. Heat 2 tablespoons of the oil in a heavy based pan or wok. Add the strips of pork and stir-fry over high heat for 2-3 minutes. Remove the meat and keep warm.
3. Heat the remaining oil and stir-fry the garlic, ginger, onions and nuts for 2 minutes. Add the red pepper and bean-sprouts and stir-fry for a further 2 minutes.
4. Return the pork to the pan, pour on the sauce, bring to the boil, stirring, lower the heat and simmer for 2 minutes.

# MUSHROOMS AND LIVER PROVENÇAL

*Serves 4*

450 g (1 lb) lamb's liver, sliced
25 g (1 oz) wholewheat flour
salt
freshly ground black pepper
1 teaspoon fresh marjoram
25 g (1 oz) soft margarine
1 tablespoon sunflower oil
1 garlic clove, peeled and crushed
1 medium onion, peeled and thinly sliced
1 green pepper, cored, seeded and sliced
1 red pepper, cored, seeded and sliced
100 g (4 oz) mushrooms, sliced
4 large tomatoes, skinned and sliced
2 teaspoons soft dark brown sugar
1 teaspoon red wine vinegar
350 g (12 oz) green noodles

*Preparation time: 15 minutes*
*Cooking time: 20 minutes*

# VEAL KEBABS WITH GINGER DRESSING

*Serves 4*

450 g (1 lb) leg of veal, trimmed of excess fat and
cut into 2.5 cm (1 inch) cubes
1 green pepper, cored, seeded and cut into
2.5 cm (1 inch) squares
1 red pepper, cored, seeded and cut into
2.5 cm (1 inch) squares
2 medium courgettes, cut into 1 cm
(½ inch) slices
100 g (4 oz) small button mushrooms
4 bay leaves
1 lemon or orange, quartered, to garnish
*Marinade:*
3 tablespoons sunflower oil
1 tablespoon red wine vinegar
2 teaspoons grated orange rind
1 tablespoon orange juice
2.5 cm (1 inch) piece fresh root ginger, peeled and
chopped
½ teaspoon ground ginger
salt
freshly ground black pepper

*Preparation time: 25 minutes, plus marinating*
*Cooking time: 15 minutes*

*1.* Mix together the marinade ingredients.
*2.* On 4 skewers, thread the veal, peppers,
courgettes, mushrooms and bay leaves, alternating the colours and ending with a bay leaf.
*3.* Place the skewers in a shallow dish, pour over
the marinade and turn the skewers in the mixture. Cover and set aside for about 2 hours.
*4.* Heat the grill to moderate. Drain the skewers
and grill for 10-12 minutes, turning frequently
and basting them with the marinade. Garnish
with the lemon or orange wedges. Serve immediately with brown rice.

# VEAL WITH CHILLI

*Serves 4*

225 g (8 oz) dried red kidney beans, soaked
overnight and drained
1 small onion, peeled and sliced
1 bay leaf
1 bouquet garni
1 tablespoon sunflower oil
2 medium onions, peeled and sliced
1 garlic clove, peeled and finely chopped
450 g (1 lb) minced pie veal
1 tablespoon wholewheat flour
salt
freshly ground black pepper
1 teaspoon dried oregano
1 teaspoon paprika
1 teaspoon chilli powder (or to taste)
2 red peppers, cored, seeded and thinly sliced
350 g (12 oz) tomatoes, skinned and sliced
300 ml (½ pint) chicken stock

*Preparation time: 20 minutes, plus soaking overnight*
*Cooking time: 2 hours*

1. Put the kidney beans, onion, bay leaf and bouquet garni into a pan, cover with water, bring to the boil and fast-boil for 15-20 minutes. Lower the heat and simmer for 1 hour. Drain. Remove the bouquet garni and the bay leaf.

2. Heat the oil in a flameproof casserole and fry the onion and garlic over a moderate heat for 2 minutes, stirring once or twice. Add the meat, stir well and cook for 5 minutes. Stir in the flour, salt, pepper, oregano, paprika and chilli powder and cook for 2 minutes. Add the peppers, tomatoes and kidney bean mixture and pour on the stock.

3. Bring to the boil, cover the dish and simmer for 45 minutes, stirring occasionally. Taste and adjust the seasoning if necessary. **F**

**F** *Freeze the dish for up to 2 months. Thaw from frozen in a pan on top of the cooker.*

# RED PEPPER CHICKEN

*Serves 4*

4 breasts of chicken, skinned
25 g (1 oz) soft margarine
2 tablespoons sunflower oil
12 black olives, to garnish
*Sauce:*
1 tablespoon sunflower oil
1 medium onion, peeled and finely chopped
2 garlic cloves, peeled and finely chopped
2 red peppers, cored, seeded and thinly sliced
450 g (1 lb) tomatoes, skinned and sliced
1 tablespoon tomato purée
2 teaspoons red wine vinegar
4 tablespoons green olives, stuffed with pimentoes, sliced
1 teaspoon soft dark brown sugar
salt
freshly ground black pepper
pinch of ground cumin
2 tablespoons chopped parsley

*Preparation time: 20 minutes*
*Cooking time: 50 minutes*

1. Dry the chicken breasts on paper towels. Heat the margarine and oil in a frying pan and fry the chicken over a moderate heat for 5 minutes on each side. Remove the chicken from the pan and keep it warm.

2. To make the sauce, heat the oil in a pan and fry the onion and garlic over a moderate heat for 3 minutes, stirring once or twice. Add the peppers and cook for 2 minutes. Then add the tomatoes, tomato purée, vinegar, olives and sugar and season well with salt, pepper and cumin. Bring the sauce to the boil and simmer, uncovered, for 15 minutes.

3. Return the chicken to the pan and simmer for 15-20 minutes, until it is cooked. Stir in the parsley, taste the sauce and adjust the seasoning if needed.

4. Garnish the dish with the black olives. This dish is good served with wholewheat pasta shells or rice, and a green salad.

*From the left: Veal kebabs with ginger dressing; Veal with chilli; Red pepper chicken.*

# CHICKEN IN A BRICK

*Serves 4-6*

1.5 kg (3¼ lb) oven-ready chicken
1 tablespoon lemon juice
*Filling:*
25 g (1 oz) soft margarine
1 small onion, peeled and finely chopped
1 celery stick, finely chopped
100 g (4 oz) dried pears, chopped
50 g (2 oz) fresh wholewheat breadcrumbs
50 g (2 oz) Brazil nuts, chopped
1 teaspoon grated lemon rind
salt
freshly ground black pepper
1 small egg, beaten
parsley sprigs, to garnish

*Preparation time: 35 minutes*
*Cooking time: 1 hour 50 minutes*
*Oven: 220°C, 425°F, Gas Mark 7 (do not preheat)*

*Although a chicken brick is used in this recipe, you can, of course, cook the chicken with dried pear stuffing in a roasting pan in the oven in the normal way.*

*1.* Soak the chicken brick in warm water for 15 minutes. To make the filling, melt the margarine and fry the onion and celery together over moderate heat for 3 minutes, stirring once or twice. Remove from the heat and stir in the pears, breadcrumbs, Brazil nuts and lemon rind and season with salt and pepper. Beat in the egg. **F**

*2.* Wipe the chicken inside and out with a damp cloth. Spoon the filling into the cavity and tie the legs together with string. Sprinkle the lemon juice over the bird.

*3.* Line the chicken brick with greaseproof paper. Place the bird in the brick, cover with greaseproof paper and put on the lid.

*4.* Place the chicken brick in a cold oven and set the heat as indicated. Cook for 1¾ hours, or until the chicken is cooked. To test, pierce the thickest part of the thigh with a fine skewer: the juices should run clear.

*5.* Transfer the chicken to a heated serving dish and garnish with parsley sprigs. Pour off the juices from the brick and serve separately.

**F** *Freeze the filling for up to 1 month. Thaw completely before using.*

# ALMOND-COATED TURKEY

*Serves 4*

4 slices breast of turkey, about 100-125 g
(4-5 oz each)
50 g (2 oz) chopped blanched almonds
25 g (1 oz) soft margarine
1 tablespoon sunflower oil
2 teaspoons wholewheat flour
150 ml (¼ pint) plain unsweetened yogurt
2 tablespoons chicken stock
1 tablespoon grated orange rind
4 tablespoons orange juice
salt
freshly ground black pepper
pinch of ground cinnamon
2 oranges, segmented, to garnish

*Preparation time: 15 minutes*
*Cooking time: 15 minutes*

1. Coat the turkey in the chopped almonds, pressing the nuts well into the meat.
2. Heat the margarine and oil in a frying pan and fry the turkey slices over a moderate heat for 5 minutes on each side. Remove them from the pan and keep them warm.
3. In a small pan, stir the flour to a paste with a little of the yogurt, then pour on the remainder and bring to the boil, stirring. Simmer for 3 minutes.
4. Stir the stock, orange rind and juice into the frying pan and bring to the boil. Pour on the yogurt, season with salt, pepper and cinnamon and simmer for 1 minute.
5. Pour the sauce on to a heated serving dish. Place the turkey slices on the sauce and garnish with the orange segments.

# HARE WITH JUNIPER

*Serves 4*

1 kg (2¼ lb) hare pieces
15 g (½ oz) soft margarine
2 tablespoons sunflower oil
150 ml (¼ pint) dry cider
150 ml (¼ pint) plain unsweetened yogurt
2 teaspoons wholewheat flour
1 tablespoon chopped parsley, to garnish
*Marinade:*
2 tablespoons sunflower oil
150 ml (¼ pint) red wine
10 juniper berries, crushed
strip of thinly pared orange rind
salt
freshly ground black pepper
1 small onion, peeled and sliced
2 bay leaves

*Preparation time: 40 minutes, plus marinating*
*Cooking time: 1¼ hours*

1. Mix together the marinade ingredients. Pour the marinade into a strong polythene bag and add the pieces of hare. Tie the bag securely, turn it from side to side and place it on a plate. Leave in the refrigerator for at least 4 hours, or overnight.
2. Strain the hare, reserving the marinade. Cut the flesh from the bones and dry the meat on paper towels.
3. Heat the margarine and oil in a flameproof casserole. Fry the hare over a moderate heat until it is evenly browned on all sides. Pour on the strained marinade and the cider, season with salt and pepper and bring to the boil.
4. Cover the casserole and simmer gently for 45 minutes.
5. Pour a little of the yogurt on to the flour, stirring constantly, then stir in the remainder. In a small pan, bring the yogurt to the boil, stirring, and simmer for 3 minutes.
6. Stir the yogurt into the casserole and simmer for 15 minutes, or until the meat is tender. Garnish the dish with the parsley. Serve with rice or noodles.

*Clockwise from the left: Chicken in a brick; Hare with juniper; Almond-coated turkey.*

# FISH DISHES

Fish of all kinds is the perfect wholefood. It is high in protein and packed with minerals and vitamins, yet relatively low – in comparison with meat – in both fat and calories, and so deserves equally high ranking as a main-dish ingredient. Fish farms apart, it is the only true wild fresh food that we have. It is also easier to digest than meat and, generally, it does not take so long to cook.

The more oily fish, such as herring, mackerel, trout and sardines are well complemented, as our recipes show, by fruit, vegetables, spices and fibre. Baked bramley trout has an apple filling, Baked herrings in ginger sauce, a piquant Chinese-inspired sauce, whilst Mackerel with oranges combines fruit, vegetables and fibre in its stuffing of oranges, celery, spring onions and brown rice.

White fish combines particularly well with high-fibre foods, too. A fish pie takes on a new personality when the pastry crust consists of crisp and crunchy wholewheat shortcrust, and both creamy fish soufflés and rolled fillets are given added flavour, 'bite' and valuable dietary fibre with the addition of sweetcorn, the ingredient New Englanders selected as the best complement to their sea harvest.

# TROUT VINAIGRETTE

*Serves 4*

50 g (2 oz) soft margarine
1 large onion, peeled and thinly sliced into rings
1 green pepper, cored, seeded and thinly sliced
into rings
1 red pepper, cored, seeded and thinly sliced
into rings
4 medium trout, gutted and cleaned
2 teaspoons red wine vinegar
6 tablespoons plain unsweetened yogurt
2 hard-boiled eggs, finely chopped
salt
freshly ground black pepper

*Preparation time: 20 minutes*
*Cooking time: 30 minutes*

*1.* Melt half the margarine in a non-stick frying
pan and fry the onion and pepper rings over a
moderate heat for 5 minutes, stirring often.
Remove them with a slotted spoon and set
aside to keep warm.

*2.* Melt the remaining margarine and fry the trout
for 5-6 minutes on each side, until golden

brown. Transfer the fish to a heated serving
dish and keep warm.

*3.* Add the vinegar, yogurt and chopped egg to
the pan, season with salt and pepper and stir
well. Liquidize the sauce or press it through a
sieve to make it smooth, then reheat it gently.

*4.* Return the fish and vegetable rings to the pan
and heat through. Wholemeal bread and a
green salad are good accompaniments to this
summer dish.

# MACKEREL WITH ORANGES

*Serves 4*

3 oranges
25 g (1 oz) soft margarine
2 spring onions, finely chopped
2 tender celery sticks, finely chopped
75 g (3 oz) cooked brown rice
½ teaspoon dried rosemary, crumbled
40 g (1½ oz) walnuts, chopped
salt
freshly ground black pepper
4 small mackerel, cleaned and boned
1 small orange, peeled and cut into
thin slices, to serve

# BAKED BRAMLEY TROUT

*Serves 4*

4 medium trout, cleaned
6 tablespoons dry cider
2 bay leaves
*Filling:*
1 tablespoon vegetable oil
1 small onion, peeled and finely chopped
75 g (3 oz) wholewheat breadcrumbs
1 large cooking apple, peeled, cored and finely chopped
1 teaspoon grated lemon rind
1 tablespoon lemon juice
1 tablespoon chopped parsley
1 teaspoon dried thyme
1 tablespoon sunflower seeds
3 tablespoons milk
salt
freshly ground black pepper

*Preparation time: 25 minutes*
*Cooking time: 30 minutes*
*Oven: 180°C, 350°F, Gas Mark 4*

1. Heat the oil in a small pan and fry the onion over moderate heat for 3 minutes, stirring once or twice.
2. Remove from the heat and stir in all the remaining filling ingredients. **F**
3. Spoon the filling into the cavities in the trout.
4. Place the fish head-to-tail in a greased, shallow baking dish, season with salt and pepper and pour over the cider. Add the bay leaves.
5. Bake the fish in a preheated oven for 25 minutes, basting with the cider from time to time. Serve with small potatoes boiled in their skins and a green vegetable.

**F** *Freeze the filling for up to 1 month. Thaw for 3 hours at room temperature or overnight in the refrigerator.*

*Preparation time: 30 minutes*
*Cooking time: 45 minutes*
*Oven: 190°C, 375°F, Gas Mark 5*

1. Grate the rind and squeeze the juice of 1 orange. Peel the second and chop the flesh. Thinly slice the third and reserve to garnish.
2. Melt the margarine in a small pan and fry the onion and celery over moderate heat for 3 minutes, stirring once or twice.
3. Remove from the heat and stir in the rice, rosemary, orange rind, chopped orange flesh, half the juice and the walnuts and season with salt and pepper.
4. Pack the filling into the fish and reshape.
5. Cut 4 pieces of foil about 30 × 18 cm (12 × 7 inches) and grease the centre. Place a mackerel on each piece, make 3 diagonal slashes across the top, season with salt and pepper and sprinkle on the remaining orange juice. Close the foil, sealing the edges completely.
6. Place the foil parcels on a baking tray and bake for 40 minutes. Serve with the orange slices. Green salad with a sharp, lemony dressing is a good accompaniment.

*From the left: Trout vinaigrette; Mackerel with oranges; Baked Bramley trout.*

# COD AND SWEETCORN SOUFFLÉ

*Serves 4*

4 tablespoons fresh wholewheat breadcrumbs
350 g (12 oz) cod fillet
350 ml (12 fl oz) milk
1 bay leaf
50 g (2 oz) soft margarine
25 g (1 oz) wholewheat flour
25 g (1 oz) grated Parmesan cheese
100 g (4 oz) frozen sweetcorn, thawed
3 tablespoons double cream
salt
freshly ground black pepper
3 egg yolks
4 egg whites, stiffly beaten
pinch of paprika

*Preparation time: 30 minutes*
*Cooking time: 1 hour*
*Oven: 190°C, 375°F, Gas Mark 5*

*1.* Grease a 600 ml (1 pint) soufflé dish and sprinkle in the breadcrumbs to distribute them evenly.

*2.* Poach the fish in the milk with the bay leaf for 10 minutes. Drain the fish, reserving the liquor. Discard the bay leaf. Skin and flake the fish and remove any bones.

*3.* Melt the margarine in a small pan and stir in the flour. Pour in the fish liquor, stirring constantly until the sauce has thickened. Remove from the heat and leave to cool.

*4.* Stir in the cheese, sweetcorn and cream and season with salt and pepper. Beat in the egg yolks one at a time. Fold in the egg whites.

*5.* Pour the mixture into the prepared dish. Bake in a preheated oven for 40 minutes until the soufflé is well risen and golden brown. Serve at once, sprinkled with the paprika. Green salad makes a good balance of colour and texture.

*From the left: Cod and sweetcorn soufflé; Baked herrings in ginger sauce; Ocean rolls.*

# OCEAN ROLLS

*Serves 4*

8 small plaice fillets, skinned
salt
freshly ground black pepper
1 tablespoon lemon juice
1 tablespoon chopped parsley, to garnish
lemon slices, to garnish
*Filling:*
15 g (½ oz) soft margarine
4 rashers streaky bacon, rind removed, chopped
100 g (4 oz) mushrooms, finely chopped
50 g (2 oz) fresh wholewheat breadcrumbs
125 g (5 oz) frozen sweetcorn, thawed
1 tablespoon chopped parsley

*Preparation time: 20 minutes*
*Cooking time: 30 minutes*
*Oven: 200°C, 400°F, Gas Mark 6*

*1.* Melt the margarine and fry the bacon over moderate heat for 3-4 minutes. Stir in the mushrooms and cook for 2 minutes. Remove

from the heat. Stir in the breadcrumbs, sweet-corn and parsley and the salt and pepper.

2. Season the fillets with salt, pepper and lemon juice. Lay them skinned side up, divide the filling between them and roll up. Tie securely with fine twine.

3. Place the rolled fish in a greased, shallow baking dish. Cover with foil and bake in a preheated oven for 20 minutes. Remove strings and garnish with parsley and lemon slices.

# BAKED HERRINGS IN GINGER SAUCE

*Serves 4*

4 herrings, cleaned and boned
2 medium carrots, scraped, cut into matchstick strips
2 celery sticks, cut into matchstick strips
1 red pepper, cored, seeded and thinly sliced
1 green pepper, cored, seeded and thinly sliced
1 large onion, peeled and thinly sliced

*Sauce:*
2 tablespoons red wine vinegar
1 tablespoon soy sauce
2 tablespoons dry sherry
2 tablespoons clear honey
3 tablespoons water
1 teaspoon ground ginger
2 teaspoons cornflour
freshly ground black pepper
pinch of cayenne
2.5 cm (1 inch) piece fresh ginger root, peeled and finely chopped

*Preparation time: 15 minutes, plus marinating*
*Cooking time: 35-40 minutes*
*Oven: 190°C, 375°F, Gas Mark 5.*

1. Mix together the sauce ingredients.
2. Place the fish in a shallow baking dish, pour over the sauce, cover and leave for at least 2 hours to marinate.
3. Turn the fish in the sauce. Add the carrots, celery, peppers and onion and cover with foil.
4. Bake in a preheated oven for 35-40 minutes and serve immediately.

# SALMON STEAKS WITH ORANGE SAUCE

*Serves 4*

2 tablespoons orange juice
4 salmon steaks, about 100 g (4 oz) each
freshly ground black pepper
vegetable oil, for brushing
25 g (1 oz) butter, melted
asparagus tips, to serve
*Sauce:*
1 large egg
pinch of mustard powder
salt
freshly ground black pepper
2 teaspoons grated orange rind
1 tablespoon orange juice
120 ml (4 fl oz) sunflower oil

*Preparation time: 10 minutes, plus marinating*
*Cooking time: 10 minutes*

1. Sprinkle the orange juice over the salmon steaks, season with pepper and set aside at room temperature for at least 15 minutes.
2. Heat the grill to high and brush the grill rack with oil. Brush the salmon steaks with half the melted butter and grill for 4 minutes. Turn the steaks, brush them with the remaining butter and grill for 5 minutes on the second side.
3. To make the sauce, put all the ingredients except the oil in a blender. Blend for 2-3 seconds. Then, with the machine running, pour in the oil gradually. Taste the sauce and adjust the seasoning if necessary.
4. Serve the fish with the sauce and asparagus.

*Below: Salmon steaks with orange sauce.*
*Right: Grey mullet in mushroom sauce.*

## GREY MULLET IN MUSHROOM SAUCE

*Serves 4*

1 grey mullet, about 1 kg (2¼ lb) or 2, about 500 g
1¼ lb each, cleaned and heads removed
3 tablespoons sunflower oil
*Sauce:*
1 large onion, peeled and thinly sliced
225 g (8 oz) tomatoes, skinned and sliced
175 g (6 oz) button mushrooms, sliced
50 g (2 oz) chopped walnuts
1 tablespoon chopped parsley
250 ml (8 fl oz) dry white wine
salt
freshly ground black pepper
coriander leaves or parsley, to garnish

*Preparation time: 15 minutes*
*Cooking time: 45 minutes*
*Oven: 200°C, 400°F, Gas Mark 6*

1. Cut 3 diagonal slashes in each side of the fish. Place the fish in a large ovenproof dish and grill under moderate heat for 5 minutes on each side. Cover the fish and keep warm.
2. Fry the onion for 3 minutes, then stir in the tomatoes and mushrooms, and cook for 5 minutes until softened.
3. Stir in the walnuts, parsley and wine, season with salt and pepper and bring to the boil. Simmer for 10 minutes.
4. Spoon the sauce over the fish and cook in a preheated oven for 15 minutes, until the fish is just firm.
5. Garnish with the coriander leaves or parsley.

# NAVARRE SARDINES

*Serves 4*

700 g (1½ lb) fresh sardines, cleaned and heads removed
2 tablespoons milk
25 g (1 oz) wholewheat flour
1 teaspoon dried tarragon
pinch of cayenne pepper
sunflower oil, for brushing
sprigs of tarragon, to garnish
*Sauce:*
2 tablespoons sunflower oil
1 medium onion, peeled and finely chopped
1 celery stick, finely chopped
1 red pepper, cored, seeded and finely chopped
2 tablespoons tomato purée
2 tablespoons red wine vinegar
1 tablespoon Worcestershire sauce
1 tablespoon soft dark brown sugar
1 teaspoon mustard
4 tablespoons orange juice
salt
freshly ground black pepper

*Preparation time: 20 minutes*
*Cooking time: 40 minutes*

1. To make the sauce, heat the oil and fry the onion, celery and pepper over moderate heat for 5 minutes, stirring often. Add the tomato purée, vinegar, Worcestershire sauce, sugar, mustard and orange juice, season with salt and pepper and bring to the boil. Simmer for 20 minutes, until the sauce thickens.

2. Brush the fish with milk and toss in flour seasoned with the tarragon and cayenne.

3. Heat the grill to moderate. Brush the grill pan with oil and grill the fish for 5-6 minutes, turning once.

4. Pour the sauce into a small bowl, stand it in the centre of a heated serving dish and arrange the fish around it. Garnish with sprigs of tarragon.

# CONFETTI COD

*Serves 4*

4 cod steaks, about 150 g (5 oz) each
4 teaspoons lemon juice
300 ml (½ pint) plain unsweetened yogurt, Greek if available
salt
freshly ground black pepper
½ teaspoon paprika
large pinch of cayenne
175 g (6 oz) frozen peeled prawns
100 g (4 oz) button mushrooms, thinly sliced
unpeeled prawns, to garnish

*Preparation time: 15 minutes*
*Cooking time: 20 minutes*
*Oven: 190°C, 375°F, Gas Mark 5*

*1.* Sprinkle the fish with half the lemon juice.

*2.* Season the yogurt with salt, pepper, paprika, cayenne and the remaining lemon juice and stir in the prawns.

*3.* Place each cod steak in the centre of a square of greased foil. Cover the fish with the mushrooms and pour on the prawn sauce. Seal up the foil to make leakproof but loose parcels.

*4.* Place the fish parcels on a baking sheet and cook in a preheated oven for 20 minutes.

*5.* To serve, slit open the parcels and garnish each one with unpeeled prawns. Rice is a good choice to serve with the fish.

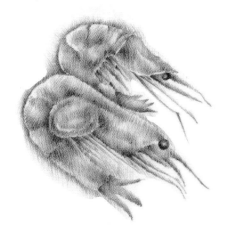

*From the left: Confetti cod; Navarre sardines; Baked fillets of sole.*

# BAKED FILLETS OF SOLE

*Serves 4*

4 small lemon or Dover soles, about 275 g (10 oz) each
1 small onion, peeled and quartered
1 small carrot, scraped and halved lengthways
1 celery stick, sliced
2 bay leaves
8 green peppercorns
1 tablespoon lemon juice
150 ml (¼ pint) dry white wine
150 ml (¼ pint) water
25 g (1 oz) butter
25 g (1 oz) flour
300 ml (½ pint) milk
3 tablespoons double cream
salt
freshly ground black pepper
pinch of ground coriander
2 kiwi fruits, peeled and sliced, to garnish

*Preparation time: 40 minutes*
*Cooking time: 1 hour*
*Oven: 180°C, 350°F, Gas Mark 4*

*1.* Skin and bone the sole, cutting each one into 4 fillets (or, if you prefer, ask the fishmonger to do it for you).

*2.* To make the stock, put the fish trimmings, onion, carrot, celery, bay leaves, peppercorns, lemon juice, wine and water into a pan. Bring to the boil, cover and simmer for 30 minutes, then strain.

*3.* Loosely roll the fish fillets, skinned side up, and place them in a shallow baking dish. Pour on the stock, cover with foil and bake in a preheated oven for 15 minutes.

*4.* Strain off the liquor and reserve. Keep the fish warm.

*5.* Melt the butter in a small pan, stir in the flour and pour on the milk and 150 ml (¼ pint) of the fish liquor, stirring constantly. Bring to the boil, still stirring, and simmer for 3 minutes. Stir in the cream and season with salt, pepper and coriander.

*6.* Arrange the fish fillets on a heated serving dish, pour over the sauce and garnish with slices of kiwi fruit.

# DEEP-DISH SEAFOOD PIE

*Serves 4*

450 g (1 lb) haddock fillets
450 ml (¾ pint) milk
1 bay leaf
6 black peppercorns
25 g (1 oz) butter
25 g (1 oz) flour
100 g (4 oz) button mushrooms, sliced
100 g (4 oz) peeled prawns
2 hard-boiled eggs, quartered
1 tablespoon chopped parsley
1 tablespoon capers
salt
freshly ground black pepper
pinch of cayenne
*Wholewheat shortcrust pastry:*
225 g (8 oz) wholewheat flour
salt
150 g (5 oz) soft margarine
50 g (2 oz) oat flakes
cold water, to mix
1 egg, beaten, for brushing

*Preparation time: 50 minutes, plus chilling pastry*
*Cooking time: 45 minutes*
*Oven: 200°C, 400°F, Gas Mark 6*

1. To make the pastry, sift the flour and salt and mix in the margarine. Stir in the oat flakes and use just enough cold water to form a dough. Knead the dough lightly. Wrap in cling film or foil and chill for at least 30 minutes.
2. Poach the fish in the milk with the bay leaf and peppercorns for 10 minutes. Drain the fish, reserving the milk. Skin and flake the fish and remove any bones.
3. Melt the butter. Stir in the flour and gradually pour on the fish liquor, stirring constantly. Simmer the sauce for 3 minutes. Remove from the heat and cool a little.
4. Carefully stir the flaked fish, prawns, mushrooms, eggs, parsley and capers into the sauce and season with salt, pepper and cayenne.
5. Turn the fish mixture into a 1 litre (1¾ pint) pie dish.
6. Roll out the pastry on a lightly floured board. Cut off a strip and place it around the rim of the dish. Dampen the rim. Place the pastry on top, trim and flute the edges. Brush the pastry top with beaten egg.
7. Reroll the pastry trimmings and cut simple fish shapes. Place them in 'shoal formation' on the pie and brush with beaten egg. Make a vent in the centre.
8. Bake the pie in a preheated oven for 25-30 minutes. Serve hot.

# STIR-FRIED PRAWNS

*Serves 4*

225 g (8 oz) broccoli florets, quartered
salt
3 tablespoons dry white wine
1 tablespoon cornflour
1 egg white
350 g (12 oz) peeled prawns
4 tablespoons sunflower oil
2 spring onions, thinly sliced
1 garlic clove, peeled and finely chopped
1 slice fresh root ginger, peeled and finely chopped
3 medium courgettes, thinly sliced diagonally
*Sauce:*
3 tablespoons dry sherry
1 tablespoon tomato purée
1 teaspoon sugar
3 tablespoons soy sauce

*Preparation time: 30 minutes*
*Cooking time: 10 minutes*

*Careful preparation is of great importance to the appearance of the dish. Slice the vegetables so that they are of even sizes. You can do this, and mix the sauce, in advance and store each ingredient in the refrigerator in separate lidded containers for up to 3-4 hours.*

1. Mix together the sauce ingredients.
2. Blanch the broccoli in boiling, salted water for 1 minute. Drain, plunge at once into cold water, then drain again.
3. Stir the wine into the cornflour to make a paste, then stir in the egg white. Pour this mixture over the prawns.
4. Heat the oil in a large, heavy-based frying pan or wok and stir-fry the onions, garlic and ginger for 1 minute. Add the prawns and stir-fry for 1 minute, then add the courgettes and continue stirring for 2 minutes.
5. Pour on the sauce, add the broccoli and stir for 2 minutes. Serve at once with rice.

*From the top: Deep-dish seafood pie; Stir-fried prawns.*

# PRAWN PATHIA

*Serves 4*

2 tablespoons sunflower oil
1 medium onion, peeled and chopped
2 garlic cloves, peeled and finely chopped
1 teaspoon turmeric
½ teaspoon chilli powder
½ teaspoon ground cumin
½ teaspoon ground black pepper
¼ teaspoon ground cardamom
pinch of ground cloves
1 teaspoon salt
1 bay leaf
150 ml (¼ pint) tomato purée
450 g (1 lb) peeled prawns
150 ml (¼ pint) boiling water
1 tablespoon lemon juice
65 g (2½ oz) creamed coconut
1 teaspoon garam masala
2 tablespoons chopped coriander leaves, or parsley
unpeeled prawns, to garnish

*Preparation time: 15 minutes*
*Cooking time: 20 minutes*

1. Heat the oil in a large saucepan and fry the onion over moderate heat for 3 minutes, stirring once or twice. Add the garlic and fry for 1 minute. Stir in the turmeric, chilli powder, cumin, pepper, cardamom, cloves, salt and bay leaf and cook for 1 minute. Stir in the tomato purée and the prawns and cook for 2 minutes.
2. Pour on the water and lemon juice and bring to the boil. Stir in the creamed coconut and garam masala and simmer for 6-7 minutes until the sauce is thick.
3. Stir in half the chopped coriander. Sprinkle the remainder over the prawns and garnish with unpeeled prawns. Rice is the traditional accompaniment to this Indian dish. A salad of thinly sliced raw courgettes tossed in plain unsweetened yogurt and mint is a cooling and refreshing contrast.

*Below: Prawn pathia.*

# TANDOORI FISH

*Serves 4*

750 g (1½ lb) haddock fillets, skinned
lemon wedges, to garnish
*Sauce:*
300 ml (½ pint) plain unsweetened yogurt
2 tablespoons lemon juice
1 small onion, peeled and finely chopped
1 tablespoon sweet paprika
½ teaspoon cayenne
1 teaspoon ground cumin
1 tablespoon tomato purée
salt
freshly ground black pepper
1 bay leaf

*Preparation time: 10 minutes, plus 2 hours marinating*
*Cooking time: 15 minutes*

*If you use home made yogurt it is best to stabilize it before heating it, at stage 3. Stir it into 2 teaspoons flour to make a paste then heat it slowly, stirring constantly.*

1. Mix together all the sauce ingredients.
2. Place the fish in a shallow dish. Pour over half the sauce, cover and leave in the refrigerator to marinate for at least 2 hours. Refrigerate the reserved sauce.
3. Heat the grill to moderate and line the grill pan with foil. Remove the fish and grill for 6 minutes on each side. Heat the sauce through gently in a small saucepan.
4. Garnish the fish with lemon wedges and serve the sauce separately. Serve with rice, grilled poppadoms and chutneys.

*Above: Tandoori fish.*

# PASTA, PULSES & GRAINS

As a health food, pasta has only recently emerged due to the realisation that it isn't the pasta itself that makes us fat – it's the quantities of meat, cream and butter that we eat with it.

Choose wholewheat pasta and you have a product that retains the wheat germ and bran (ordinary pasta contains 0.3 per cent dietary fibre, whilst wholewheat kinds have a minimum of 10 per cent) and experiment with dressings and sauces made with low-fat cheeses, yogurt, crisp and lightly cooked vegetables and fresh herbs.

Pulses (dried peas and beans) and grains (the seed of cereal plants) complement each other perfectly. Whilst pulses contain iron, B group vitamins and a high amount of proteins, they lack the amino acids of cereal foods. Thus a dish of black beans and rice (or indeed beans on wholemeal toast) comprises a full complement of protein.

Pre-soaking shortens the cooking time of pulses and grains considerably. Soak pulses overnight in cold water, or by the 'short' method: put them in cold water, bring to the boil, then soak for 1 hour. **Fast-boil all kidney beans for 15-20 minutes to dispel harmful toxins** and cook all pulses until they are only just tender.

# BUCKWHEAT SPAGHETTI WITH SPICED CHICKEN

*Serves 4*

225 g (8 oz) buckwheat spaghetti
salt
40 g (1½ oz) soft margarine
1 medium onion, peeled and finely chopped
1 garlic clove, peeled and finely chopped
1 teaspoon ground coriander
½ teaspoon ground cardamom
2 tablespoons wholewheat flour
150 ml (¼ pint) plain unsweetened yogurt
450 ml (¾ pint) chicken stock
350 g (12 oz) cooked chicken, diced
2 egg yolks
1 tablespoon chopped fresh parsley
100 g (4 oz) button mushrooms, thinly sliced
40 g (1½ oz) fresh wholewheat breadcrumbs
25 g (1 oz) grated Parmesan cheese
sprig of parsley, to garnish

*Preparation time: 20 minutes*
*Cooking time: 1 hour*
*Oven: 180°C, 350°F, Gas Mark 4*

1. Cook the spaghetti in plenty of boiling, salted water for about 12 minutes, or according to the directions on the packet, until it is just tender. Drain, refresh in hot water, and drain again.
2. Melt the margarine and fry the onion over moderate heat for 3 minutes, stirring frequently. Add the garlic, coriander and cardamom and cook for 1 minute. Stir in the flour and cook for 1 minute. Remove the pan from the heat and gradually stir in the yogurt, then the stock. Simmer for 3 minutes. Remove from the heat and allow to cool a little.
3. Stir in the chicken, egg yolks and parsley.
4. Spread half the spaghetti in a greased, shallow baking dish and cover with half the chicken sauce. Arrange the mushrooms on top, then. cover with the remaining spaghetti and then the sauce. Mix the breadcrumbs and cheese and sprinkle over the top.
5. Put the dish on a baking tray, place in a pre-heated oven and bake for 45 minutes. Serve hot, garnished with a sprig of parsley.

*From the top: Mushroom and ham lasagne; Buckwheat spaghetti with spiced chicken.*

# MUSHROOM AND HAM LASAGNE

*Serves 4-6*

225 g (8 oz) wholewheat lasagne
salt
2 tablespoons olive oil
1 large onion, peeled and chopped
225 g (8 oz) button mushrooms, thinly sliced
1 tablespoon flour
1 tablespoon lemon juice
300 ml (½ pint) plain unsweetened yogurt
freshly ground black pepper
75 g (3 oz) chopped walnuts
100 g (4 oz) lean ham, cut into matchstick strips
1 tablespoon chopped fresh parsley
*Sauce:*
300 ml (½ pint) plain unsweetened yogurt
175 g (6 oz) Wensleydale cheese, grated
6 tablespoons wholewheat or wholemeal
breadcrumbs

*Preparation time: 40 minutes*
*Cooking time: 1 hour*
*Oven: 190°C, 375°F, Gas Mark 5*

1. Cook the lasagne sheets in plenty of boiling, salted water for about 15 minutes, or according to the directions on the packet, until it is just tender, stirring occasionally. Drain, rinse in cold water and drain again. Pat the sheets dry with kitchen paper.
2. Heat the oil and fry the onion over moderate heat for 3 minutes, stirring frequently. Add the mushrooms and cook for 2 minutes. Stir in the flour and cook for 1 minute. Remove the pan from the heat and gradually stir in the lemon juice and yogurt. Cook, stirring, until the mixture thickens, then season. Simmer for 2 minutes. Stir in the walnuts, ham and parsley and remove from the heat.
3. Pour a layer of this sauce into a greased, shallow baking dish. Cover with sheets of lasagne and continue making layers, finishing with a layer of lasagne.
4. For the sauce, stir the yogurt and half the cheese together and pour over the dish. Sprinkle over the remaining cheese mixed with the breadcrumbs.
5. Stand the dish on a baking sheet. Place in a preheated oven and bake for 25-30 minutes, or until the top is deep brown and the sauce bubbling.

# CANNELLONI WITH SPINACH FILLING

*Serves 4-6*

750 g (1½ lb) fresh spinach, stalks removed
50 g (2 oz) butter
225 g (8 oz) Ricotta or cottage cheese, sieved
75 g (3 oz) grated Parmesan cheese
salt
freshly ground black pepper
pinch of grated nutmeg
2 large eggs
12 large cannelloni tubes
25 g (1 oz) flour
300 ml (½ pint) milk
4 tablespoons bran cereal

*Preparation time: 50 minutes*
*Cooking time: 1 hour*
*Oven: 180°C, 350°F, Gas Mark 4*

1. Wash the spinach and cook in the water clinging to the leaves in a large pan for 12 minutes over moderate heat. Stir frequently. Drain the spinach in a colander, pressing out all moisture. Chop the spinach finely.
2. Melt half the butter in a pan, add the spinach and stir well. Remove from the heat.
3. Beat the sieved cottage cheese and half the Parmesan cheese into the spinach and season with salt, pepper and nutmeg. Beat in the eggs. Set aside to cool.
4. Cook the cannelloni tubes in plenty of boiling, salted water for about 10 minutes, or according to the directions on the packet, until they are just tender. Drain, refresh in cold water, and drain again. Dry thoroughly with kitchen paper. Set aside to cool.
5. Melt the remaining butter in a pan, stir in the flour, and cook for 1 minute. Remove from the heat and gradually stir in the milk, stirring constantly. Bring to the boil, season with salt and pepper and simmer for 5 minutes. Taste and adjust the seasoning if necessary.
6. Use a piping bag (but no nozzle) to fill the cannelloni tubes with the spinach mixture.
7. Place the filled cannelloni in a greased, shallow baking dish. Pour over the sauce and sprinkle with the remaining cheese mixed with the cereal.
8. Stand the dish on a baking sheet. Place in a preheated oven and bake for 35-40 minutes, or until the topping is dark brown and crusty.

# CARAMELLI WITH BASIL SAUCE

*Serves 4*

350 g (12 oz) wholewheat caramelli shells, or other pasta shapes
salt
75 g (3 oz) fresh basil leaves
4 tablespoons olive oil
3 garlic cloves, peeled and crushed
50 g (2 oz) pine kernels, or blanched slivered almonds
50 g (2 oz) grated Parmesan cheese
25 g (1 oz) softened butter
freshly ground black pepper

*Preparation time: 15 minutes*
*Cooking time: 12 minutes*

# FLAMED TAGLIATELLE WITH YOGURT

*Serves 4*

350 g (12 oz) wholewheat tagliatelle, or other
pasta shapes
salt
50 g (2 oz) butter
3 tablespoons brandy
150 ml (¼ pint) plain unsweetened yogurt
60 g (2½ oz) grated Parmesan cheese
freshly ground black pepper
50 g (2 oz) walnut halves, to garnish

*Preparation time: 10 minutes*
*Cooking time: 10 minutes*

1. Cook the tagliatelle in plenty of boiling, salted water for about 10 minutes, or according to the directions on the packet, until it is just tender. Drain, refresh in hot water, and drain again.
2. Melt the butter in a pan and toss the tagliatelle to coat thoroughly. Pour on the brandy, stir well and light it, to burn off the alcohol.
3. Stir in the yogurt and cheese, and season with plenty of black pepper. Garnish with the walnuts and serve at once.

*This sauce, made with fresh basil leaves, is known as pesto, and originated in Genoa. You can grow basil during the summer in a greenhouse or on a sunny windowsill. However, if you do not have a plentiful supply, experiment with other herbs. Both marjoram and mint make interesting – though entirely different – substitutes.*

1. Cook the pasta in plenty of boiling, salted water for about 12 minutes, or according to the directions on the packet, until it is just tender. Drain, refresh in hot water and drain again, tossing to ensure that no water is trapped inside. Keep hot.
2. To make the sauce, liquidize the herb leaves, oil, garlic and nuts in a blender. Scrape out the mixture, beat in the cheese and butter and season with pepper.
3. Spoon the sauce over the hot pasta and serve at once, as an accompaniment to meat and poultry, or on its own.

*Clockwise from top right: Flamed tagliatelle with yogurt; Caramelli with basil sauce; Cannelloni with spinach filling.*

# VERMICELLI FLAN

*Serves 4*

225 g (8 oz) vermicelli
salt
25 g (1 oz) butter
2-3 tablespoons olive oil
3 medium onions, peeled and chopped
3 medium courgettes, thinly sliced
1 teaspoon dried oregano
300 ml (½ pint) plain unsweetened yogurt
50 g (2 oz) Gouda cheese, grated
2 eggs
freshly ground black pepper
2 large tomatoes, thinly sliced, to garnish

*Preparation time: 25 minutes*
*Cooking time: about 1¼ hours*
*Oven: 180°C, 350°F, Gas Mark 4*

1. Cook the vermicelli in plenty of boiling, salted water for about 12 minutes, or according to the directions given on the packet, until it is just tender. Drain, refresh in hot water, and then drain again. Return the vermicelli to the pan and toss with the butter over moderate heat until it is well coated.
2. Press the vermicelli into a greased 20 cm (8 inch) flan ring placed on a baking sheet.
3. Heat 1 tablespoon of the oil and fry the onions over moderate heat for 3 minutes, stirring frequently. Remove the onions with a draining spoon and set them aside.
4. Heat the remaining oil and fry the courgettes for 3-4 minutes, turning once, until they begin to soften. (If your pan is not a non-stick one, you will need a little more oil.) Stir in the oregano and remove from the heat.
5. Scatter the onions over the base of the 'flan' case. Arrange the courgettes on top.
6. Beat the yogurt, cheese and eggs together and season with salt and pepper. Pour over the vegetables.
7. Place in a preheated oven and bake for 40-45 minutes, or until the filling is set. Serve hot, garnished with tomato rings.

# MACARONI WITH PEPPER SAUCE

*Serves 4*

350 g (12 oz) wholewheat short-cut macaroni
salt
4 tablespoons olive oil
1 large onion, peeled and sliced
3 garlic cloves, peeled and finely chopped
2 green peppers, cored, seeded and sliced into matchstick strips
1 yellow pepper, cored, seeded and sliced into matchstick strips
1 red pepper, cored, seeded and sliced into matchstick strips
350 g (12 oz) tomatoes, peeled and sliced
2 tablespoons chopped fresh parsley
black olives, to decorate
grated cheese, to serve (optional)

*Preparation time: 30 minutes*
*Cooking time: 15 minutes*

1. Cook the macaroni in plenty of boiling, salted water for about 12 minutes, or according to the directions on the packet, until it is just tender. Drain, refresh in hot water, and drain again. Keep hot.
2. Heat the oil and fry the onion, garlic and peppers over moderately high heat for about 5 minutes, or until they just begin to soften. Add the tomatoes, stir well and simmer for 10 minutes. Stir in half the parsley.
3. Turn the macaroni into a heated serving dish, pour on the sauce and toss well. Garnish with the black olives and the remaining parsley and serve with grated cheese in a separate dish.

*From the left: Vermicelli flan; Macaroni with pepper sauce; Pasta twists with mussels.*

# PASTA TWISTS WITH MUSSELS

*Serves 4*

1 kg (2 lb) mussels
300 ml (½ pint) water
150 ml (¼ pint) dry white wine
· 1 bouquet garni
350 g (12 oz) wholewheat twists, or other pasta shapes
salt
50 g (2 oz) butter
freshly ground black pepper
300 ml (½ pint) plain unsweetened yogurt
2 tablespoons chopped fresh parsley
lemon balm, to garnish
grated Parmesan cheese, to serve

*Preparation time: 1 hour*
*Cooking time: 30 minutes*

1. Thoroughly wash the mussels in several bowls of clean water and pull off the beards. Tap the mussels and discard any that do not close. Put them in a large pan with the water and wine, bring to the boil, cover the pan and steam for 5-6 minutes, or until the shells have opened. Drain the mussels and reserve the cooking liquid. Discard any unopened mussels.
2. Pour the liquid into a pan, add the bouquet garni, bring to the boil and fast-boil for 10 minutes, or until reduced by about two-thirds. Discard the bouquet garni.
3. Cut the mussels away from the shells, leaving about 8 in the shells for garnish.
4. Cook the pasta in plenty of boiling, salted water for about 12 minutes, or according to the directions on the packet, until it is just tender. Drain, refresh in hot water, then drain again.
5. Melt the butter in the pan, add the pasta twists and mussels and season with pepper. Toss well. Beat the reserved shellfish liquid with the yogurt, stir in the parsley and pour over the pasta. Toss well.
6. Turn the pasta into a heated dish, garnish with lemon balm and the reserved mussels in shells and serve with the Parmesan cheese.

# AUBERGINE LAYER

*Serves 4*

1 medium aubergine, thinly sliced
salt
225 g (8 oz) wholewheat short-cut macaroni
4 tablespoons olive oil
350 g (12 oz) minced steak
350 g (12 oz) tomatoes, skinned and sliced
1 teaspoon dried oregano
1 tablespoon chopped fresh parsley
freshly ground black pepper
100 g (4 oz) Feta or Wensleydale cheese, very
thinly sliced
100 g (4 oz) button mushrooms, thinly sliced
50 g (2 oz) fresh wholewheat breadcrumbs
50 g (2 oz) grated Parmesan cheese

*Preparation time: 30 minutes, plus draining*
*Cooking time: 1¼ hours*
*Oven: 180°C, 350°F, Gas Mark 4*

*1.* Put the aubergine slices in a colander over a
dish and sprinkle with salt. Leave to drain for
30 minutes, then rinse thoroughly. Drain the
slices and pat dry with kitchen paper.
*2.* Meanwhile, cook the macaroni in plenty of
boiling salted water for about 12 minutes, or
according to the directions on the packet, until
it is just tender. Drain, refresh in hot water, and
drain again.
*3.* Heat the oil in a pan and fry the aubergine
slices, a few at a time, over moderate heat for 5
minutes for each batch. Remove from the pan
as they are cooked and keep hot.
*4.* Fry the meat in the pan for 6 minutes, stirring
frequently. Stir in the tomatoes and herbs and
cook for 10 minutes. Season with salt and
pepper.
*5.* In a greased, shallow baking dish make layers
of the macaroni, aubergines, meat sauce, sliced
cheese and mushrooms, finishing with the
aubergine. Mix together the breadcrumbs and
Parmesan cheese and sprinkle over the top. ⓕ
*6.* Put the dish on a baking sheet. Place in a
preheated oven and bake for 45 minutes. Serve
hot with a green salad.

ⓕ *Freeze the uncooked dish for up to 2 months. Thaw in*
*the refrigerator overnight, or bake from frozen for 1 hour.*

*Clockwise from top left: Aubergine layer; Pasta twists*
*with broccoli spears; Green noodles with blue cheese.*

# GREEN NOODLES WITH BLUE CHEESE

*Serves 4*

350 g (12 oz) green spinach noodles, or other
pasta shapes
salt
6 rashers streaky bacon, rinded and chopped
225 g (8 oz) cottage cheese
50 g (2 oz) Roquefort cheese, crumbled
2 spring onions, thinly sliced
freshly ground black pepper

*Preparation time: 15 minutes*
*Cooking time: 15 minutes*

*1.* Cook the noodles in plenty of boiling, salted
water for 12 minutes, or according to the directions on the packet, until they are just tender.
Drain, refresh in hot water, and drain again.
Keep hot.
*2.* Fry the bacon over moderate heat until the fat
has run and the bacon is crispy. Remove with a
slotted spoon and reserve.
*3.* Toss the noodles with the cheeses and onions
and season with salt and pepper. Stir in the
chopped bacon.
*4.* Turn the noodles into a heated serving dish.
Serve at once.

# PASTA TWISTS WITH BROCCOLI SPEARS

*Serves 4*

350 g (12 oz) pasta twists, bows, or other shapes
salt
450 g (1 lb) broccoli spears
1 tablespoon olive oil
15 g (½ oz) butter
1 small onion, peeled and finely chopped
40 g (1½ oz) walnuts, roughly chopped
40 g (1½ oz) anchovy fillets, chopped
1 tablespoon chopped fresh parsley
freshly ground black pepper
25 g (1 oz) grated Parmesan cheese

*Preparation time: 20 minutes*
*Cooking time: 30 minutes*

*1.* Cook the pasta in plenty of boiling salted water

for 15 minutes, or according to the directions on the packet, until it is just tender. Drain immediately, refresh in hot water, and then drain once more.

2. Blanch the broccoli by cooking it in boiling salted water for 5 minutes. Drain, and plunge at once into cold water to prevent further cooking. Drain again.

3. Heat the oil with the butter and fry the onion over low heat for 10 minutes, stirring occasionally.

4. Next, stir in the walnuts, anchovies and broccoli and cook slowly over gentle heat for 3-4 minutes.

5. Stir in the pasta and heat through. Remove from the heat, add the parsley, season well with pepper and stir in the cheese. Serve at once. A green salad makes a good accompaniment.

## OLD-FASHIONED PEASE PUDDING

*Serves 4*

225 g (8 oz) dried yellow split peas, soaked
overnight and drained
1 small onion, peeled and quartered
1 bouquet garni
about 300 ml (½ pint) chicken stock (page 11)
1 large egg, lightly beaten
salt
freshly ground black pepper
½ teaspoon ground cumin
2 tablespoons chopped fresh parsley
parsley sprigs, to garnish

*Preparation time: overnight soaking, then 25 minutes*
*Cooking time: about 2¼ hours*

1. Put the peas in a pan with the onion, bouquet garni and chicken stock. Bring to the boil, cover and simmer for 1 hour, stirring occasionally, or until the peas are tender. Add a little more stock if the peas dry out before they are cooked.
2. Beat the peas to make a smooth purée, or liquidize them in a blender or food processor. Beat in the egg, season with salt, pepper and cumin and stir in the parsley.
3. Spoon the mixture into a greased 600 ml/1 pint pudding basin and cover with foil. Stand on a trivet in a pan of boiling water. Cover the pan and steam for 1¼ hours.
4. Turn the pudding out on to a heated serving dish and garnish with the parsley sprigs.

*From the left: Old-fashioned pease pudding; Mexican rice; Buckwheat spaghetti with almond sauce.*

# MEXICAN RICE

*Serves 4*

1 tablespoon sunflower oil
2 medium onions, peeled and sliced
1 red pepper, cored, seeded and chopped
225 g (8 oz) brown rice
600 ml (1 pint) chicken stock
8 small tomatoes, skinned and quartered
1 small avocado, stoned, peeled and cut into
1 cm (½ inch) chunks
4 eggs
4 tablespoons plain unsweetened yogurt
salt
freshly ground black pepper
2 tablespoons chopped coriander leaves, or
finely snipped chives, to garnish

*Preparation time: 20 minutes*
*Cooking time: 1 hour*

1. Heat the oil and fry the onion and pepper over moderate heat for 3 minutes, stirring frequently. Stir in the rice and cook for 1 minute. Stir in the stock and bring to the boil.
2. Cover the pan and simmer for 40 minutes.
3. Add the tomatoes and avocado, stirring in carefully to avoid breaking them up. Cover and simmer for 5 minutes.
4. Beat the eggs with the yogurt and season with salt and pepper. Pour over the rice and fork it over and over. Cook until the eggs are just set. Garnish with the coriander and serve at once.

# BUCKWHEAT SPAGHETTI WITH ALMOND SAUCE

*Serves 4*

350 g (12 oz) buckwheat spaghetti
salt
25 g (1 oz) butter
2 tablespoons chopped fresh parsley
*Sauce:*
100 g (4 oz) ground almonds
175 g (6 oz) cottage cheese, sieved
50 g (2 oz) grated Parmesan cheese
300 ml (½ pint) plain unsweetened yogurt
2 tablespoons olive oil
pinch of grated nutmeg
pinch of ground cinnamon
freshly ground black pepper
8 tablespoons blanched almonds, toasted
1 tablespoon chopped fresh parsley, to garnish

*Preparation time: 20 minutes*
*Cooking time: about 12 minutes*

1. Cook the spaghetti in plenty of boiling, salted water for about 12 minutes, or according to the directions on the packet, until it is just tender. Drain, refresh in hot water, and drain again. Return the spaghetti to the pan, toss it in the butter and parsley, cover and keep hot.
2. Mix all the sauce ingredients together except the toasted almonds and season with salt and pepper.
3. Turn the spaghetti into a heated serving dish. Stir the toasted almonds into the sauce, pour over the spaghetti and toss well. Garnish with chopped parsley and serve at once.

# CORIANDER CHICK PEA CASSEROLE

*Serves 4*

350 g (12 oz) dried chick peas, soaked overnight
and drained
1 small onion, peeled and quartered
a few parsley sprigs
2 tablespoons sunflower oil
1 large onion, peeled and sliced
2 garlic cloves, peeled and finely chopped
4 celery sticks, thinly sliced
2 medium carrots, scraped and thinly sliced
1 red pepper, cored, seeded and thinly sliced
2 teaspoons ground coriander
350 g (12 oz) tomatoes, skinned and sliced
150 ml (¼ pint) chicken stock
2 tablespoons chopped fresh coriander leaves, or
parsley
salt
freshly ground black pepper

*Preparation time: 25 minutes, plus soaking overnight*
*Cooking time: 4½ hours*
*Oven: 120°C, 250°F, Gas Mark ½*

1. Put the chick peas in a pan with the quartered onion and parsley, cover with water and bring to the boil. Cover and fast-boil for 5 minutes. Reduce the heat and simmer for 2 hours, or until the peas are tender. Drain the peas.
2. Heat the oil in a flameproof casserole and fry the sliced onion, garlic, celery, carrots, and red pepper over moderate heat for 4 minutes, stirring frequently. Stir in the ground coriander and cook for 1 minute.
3. Add the tomatoes, stock, peas, half the chopped herbs and season with salt and pepper. Bring to the boil and stir well.
4. Cover, place in a preheated oven and cook for 2 hours. Taste and adjust the seasoning if necessary. F Garnish with the remaining chopped herbs. Serve hot.

F *Cool the casserole and freeze it for up to 6 months. Thaw in the refrigerator overnight or at room temperature for 4-5 hours. You can also open-freeze the cooked and drained chick peas.*

## KIDNEY BEAN AND CHICKEN PAELLA

*Serves 6*

4 tablespoons olive oil
1 large onion, peeled and finely chopped
2 garlic cloves, peeled and crushed
2 red peppers, cored, seeded and chopped
350 g (12 oz) brown rice
900 ml (1½ pints) chicken stock
4 tablespoons dry sherry
½ teaspoon powdered saffron
2 chicken joints, skinned, boned and chopped
salt
freshly ground black pepper
225 g (8 oz) red kidney beans, cooked
100 g (4 oz) button mushrooms, sliced
100 g (4 oz) frozen peas
6-8 whole prawns, to garnish

*Preparation time: 30 minutes*
*Cooking time: 1 hour*

*1.* Heat the oil in a large frying pan and fry the onion over moderate heat for 3 minutes, stirring frequently. Add the garlic, peppers and rice, stir well and cook for 1 minute.

*2.* Stir in the chicken stock and sherry, add the saffron and chicken and season with salt and pepper. Bring to the boil, cover and simmer for 30 minutes.

*3.* Stir in the beans, mushrooms and peas, cover and simmer for a further 15 minutes, or until the rice is tender and the stock has been absorbed completely.

*4.* Season with more black pepper and serve hot.

*Left: Coriander chick pea casserole.*
*Above: Kidney bean and chicken paella.*

# FELAFEL

*Serves 4-6*

225 g (8 oz) dried soya beans, soaked overnight
and drained
1 large onion, peeled and grated
1 garlic clove, peeled and crushed
½ teaspoon ground coriander
½ teaspoon ground cumin
¼ teaspoon chilli powder
a pinch of ground cloves
salt
freshly ground black pepper
1 tablespoon tahine (sesame seed paste)
2 teaspoons lemon juice
1 egg, lightly beaten
wholewheat flour, for coating
sunflower oil, for frying
1 lemon, quartered, to serve

*Preparation time: 30 minutes, including overnight soaking*
*Cooking time: 2½ hours*

1. Cook the soya beans in boiling, unsalted water for 2 hours, or until they are tender. The actual time depends on the age and 'shelf-life' of the pulses. Drain.
2. Grind the soya beans to a paste in a food processor, or pass them through a vegetable mill.
3. Beat in the onion, garlic, coriander, cumin, chilli and ground cloves and season with salt and pepper. Beat in the tahine, lemon juice and enough of the egg to make a smooth paste.
4. Cover the paste and chill in the refrigerator for at least 30 minutes. This makes it much easier to handle.
5. Flour your hands and shape the mixture into rounds and press them into flat cakes. Dust all over with flour.
6. Heat very little oil and fry the cakes on both sides over moderate heat until brown. Serve hot, with the lemon wedges.

# BURGHUL CROQUETTES

*Serves 4*

2 medium carrots, scraped and quartered
salt
sunflower oil, for frying
2 medium onions, peeled and chopped
1 garlic clove, peeled and crushed
100 g (4 oz) burghul (cracked wheat)
6 tablespoons beef stock
2 tablespoons orange juice
2 tablespoons tomato purée
2 tablespoons chopped fresh parsley
1 teaspoon dried thyme
1 teaspoon orange rind
225 g (8 oz) ground hazelnuts
freshly ground black pepper
wholewheat flour, to coat

*Preparation time: 30 minutes*
*Cooking time: 40 minutes*

1. Cook the carrots in boiling, salted water for 15 minutes, or until they are tender. Drain and chop finely.
2. Heat 3 tablespoons of the sunflower oil and fry the onion and garlic over moderate heat for 3 minutes, stirring frequently. Add the burghul and carrot and cook, stirring, for 1-2 minutes. Add the stock, orange juice and tomato purée and stir well. Bring to the boil and simmer gently for 5 minutes.
3. Stir in the parsley, thyme, orange rind and hazelnuts and season with pepper.
4. Shape the mixture into 'sausages' and roll them in flour. ☒
5. Heat a very little oil in a pan and shallow-fry the croquettes for 15 minutes over moderate heat, turning frequently to brown evenly all over. Serve hot.

☒ *Open-freeze the croquettes, then store them in a rigid container for up to one month. Thaw at room temperature for 2-3 hours.*

*From the left: Felafel; Burghul croquettes; Oaty cauliflower cheese.*

# OATY CAULIFLOWER AND BROCCOLI CHEESE

*Serves 4*

1 small cauliflower, divided into florets
225 g (8 oz) broccoli spears
salt
300 ml (½ pint) plain unsweetened yogurt
1 tablespoon flour
75 g (3 oz) cottage cheese
175 g (6 oz) Gouda cheese, grated
freshly ground black pepper
100 g (4 oz) button mushrooms, sliced
25 g (1 oz) butter, melted
75 g (3 oz) rolled oats
25 g (1 oz) bran cereal
50 g (2 oz) chopped hazelnuts

*Preparation time: 25 minutes*
*Cooking time: 1 hour*
*Oven: 190°C, 375°F, Gas Mark 5*

1. Cook the cauliflower and broccoli in boiling, salted water for 5 minutes. Drain and plunge them at once into cold water to retain colour and prevent further cooking. Drain again.
2. Stir a little of the yogurt into the flour to make a smooth paste, then stir in the remaining yogurt. Heat the yogurt mixture slowly, stirring constantly. Stir in the cottage cheese and half the grated cheese, season with salt and pepper and remove from the heat.
3. Put the mushrooms, cauliflower and broccoli into a greased, shallow baking dish, mix them carefully, pour on the cheese sauce and mix the vegetables to coat them thoroughly.
4. Stir the butter, oats, bran cereal and nuts together and stir in the remaining cheese. Sprinkle over the dish.
5. Place in a preheated oven and bake for 45 minutes. Serve hot.

## NORTH OF THE BORDER PORRIDGE

*Serves 4*

1.2 litres (2 pints) boiling water
100 g (4 oz) medium oatmeal
about ½ teaspoon salt
*To serve:*
cold milk or buttermilk
soft light brown sugar or honey

*Preparation time: 5 minutes*
*Cooking time: 25 minutes*

*1.* Bring the water to the boil in a small pan. Sprinkle on the oatmeal, letting it trickle in a steady stream through your fingers, stirring all the time. Add the salt and stir until the mixture boils.

*2.* Simmer very gently for 20 minutes, stirring frequently to prevent lumps forming.

*3.* Serve at once with cold milk and sweetened with sugar or honey if liked.

## DRIED FRUIT MUESLI

*Makes 1 kg (2 lb)*

225 g (8 oz) rolled oats
100 g (4 oz) wheat flakes
50 g (2 oz) stabilized wheatgerm
50 g (2 oz) bran
50 g (2 oz) sunflower seeds
150 g (5 oz) mixed chopped nuts
100 g (4 oz) dried apricots, chopped
50 g (2 oz) seedless raisins
25 g (1 oz) dried banana chips
50 g (2 oz) stoned dried dates, chopped

*Preparation time: 20 minutes*

*1.* Mix all the ingredients together. Store in an airtight container.

*2.* Serve the muesli with plain unsweetened yogurt, buttermilk, skimmed or other milk or, for a delicious change, try it with unsweetened fruit juice.

## SEED AND CEREAL MUESLI

*Makes 450 g (1 lb)*

175 g (6 oz) rolled oats
50 g (2 oz) wheat flakes
40 g (1½ oz) stabilized wheatgerm
40 g (1½ oz) bran
50 g (2 oz) millet seeds
50 g (2 oz) sesame seeds
25 g (1 oz) pumpkin seeds

*Preparation time: 5 minutes*

*1.* Mix all the ingredients together and store in an airtight container.

## FRESH VEGETABLE MUESLI

*Serves 2*

1 small dessert apple, cored and thinly sliced
about 75 g (3 oz) seed and cereal muesli
1 small carrot, grated
1 celery stick, thinly sliced
2 tablespoons small cauliflower florets
2 teaspoons lemon juice
1 tablespoon chopped hazelnuts
2 tablespoons seedless raisins

*Preparation time: 10 minutes*

*1.* Toss the apple slices in the lemon juice to prevent discoloration.
*2.* Mix all the ingredients together. Serve with buttermilk and top with plain unsweetened yogurt.

*From the left: North of the border porridge; Dried fruit muesli; Seed and cereal muesli; Fresh vegetable muesli.*

# AUBERGINE PILAFF

*Serves 4-6*

15 g (½ oz) butter
5 tablespoons olive oil
1 large onion, peeled and finely chopped
2 celery sticks, thinly sliced
1 garlic clove, peeled and crushed
350 g (12 oz) brown rice, washed and drained
900 ml (1½ pints) chicken stock
½ teaspoon dried thyme
salt
freshly ground black pepper
1 medium aubergine, sliced, then quartered
2 large tomatoes, skinned and sliced
25 g (1 oz) blanched almonds
50 g (2 oz) seedless raisins

*Preparation time: 25 minutes*
*Cooking time: 1 hour*
*Oven: 180°C, 350°F, Gas Mark 4*

1. Melt the butter with 1 tablespoon of the oil in a flameproof casserole and fry the onion and celery over moderate heat for 3 minutes, stirring frequently. Add the garlic and rice, stir well and cook for 1 minute.
2. Stir in the stock, add the thyme and season with salt and pepper. Bring to the boil and stir thoroughly.
3. Cover the casserole, place in a preheated oven and cook for 45 minutes, or until the rice is tender and the stock has been absorbed.
4. While the rice is cooking, heat the remaining oil in a pan and fry the aubergine and tomatoes over moderate heat for 6-7 minutes, stirring frequently, or until they are tender. Season with black pepper.
5. Stir the aubergine, tomatoes, almonds and raisins into the rice. Cover and return to the oven for 5 minutes. Serve hot.

# CHICKEN AND WHOLEWHEAT RISOTTO

*Serves 4*

225 g (8 oz) whole wheat grains
salt
25 g (1 oz) butter
2 tablespoons olive oil
1 large onion, peeled and thinly sliced
2 garlic cloves, peeled and finely chopped
1 chicken breast, skinned, boned and cubed
225 g (8 oz) mushrooms, thinly sliced
2 green peppers, cored and thinly sliced
300 ml (½ pint) chicken stock
2 tablespoons medium sherry
½ teaspoon dried oregano
freshly ground black pepper
few sprigs fresh parsley
2 tablespoons walnut halves
grated Parmesan cheese, to serve

*Preparation time: 20 minutes*
*Cooking time: 1 hour 40 minutes*

1. Partly cook the wheat grains in a large pan of boiling, salted water for 1 hour. Drain.
2. Melt the butter with the oil in a large frying pan and fry the onion and garlic over moderate heat for 3 minutes, stirring frequently. Add the partly-cooked wheat, stir well and cook for 1 minute. Stir in the chicken, mushrooms and peppers and cook for 2 minutes.
3. Stir in the stock and sherry, add the oregano and season with salt and pepper.
4. Bring to the boil, cover the pan and simmer for 30 minutes, or until the wheat is tender and the stock has been absorbed.
5. Finely chop 2-3 sprigs parsley. Stir in with the walnuts and serve at once with more sprigs of parsley. Serve the cheese separately.

*From the left: Aubergine pilaff; Chicken and wholewheat risotto; Moors and Christians.*

# MOORS AND CHRISTIANS

*Serves 4-6*

225 g (8 oz) black beans, soaked overnight and drained
2 tablespoons sunflower oil
1 medium onion, peeled and chopped
1 garlic clove, peeled and crushed
1 green pepper, cored, seeded and thinly sliced
1 red pepper, cored, seeded and thinly sliced
2 red chillis, cored, seeded and finely chopped (optional)
4 large tomatoes, skinned and sliced
salt
freshly ground black pepper
½ teaspoon chilli powder (or to taste)
225 g (8 oz) long-grain brown rice
300 ml (½ pint) chicken stock
*To garnish:*
1 tablespoon chopped fresh coriander leaves, or fresh parsley sprigs
1 avocado, stoned, peeled and sliced
1 tablespoon lemon juice

*Preparation time: 30 minutes, plus soaking overnight*
*Cooking time: 2 hours*

1. Cook the beans in fast boiling, unsalted water for 15 minutes. Reduce the heat and simmer for a further 45 minutes or until they are almost tender. Drain.
2. Heat the oil and fry the onion over moderate heat for 3 minutes, stirring frequently. Add the garlic, peppers and chillis, stir well and cook for 2 minutes.
3. Add the tomatoes, salt, pepper and chilli powder and cook for 1 minute. Add the rice, stock and beans and bring to the boil.
4. Cover the pan and simmer for 45 minutes, or until the rice is tender and the stock has been absorbed completely.
5. Garnish with the coriander leaves and the avocado slices tossed in lemon juice.

# MILLET AND BROAD BEAN PILAFF

*Serves 4-6*

225 g (8 oz) millet seeds
600 ml (1 pint) chicken stock
salt
450 g (1 lb) shelled broad beans
2 tablespoons sunflower oil
1 large onion, peeled and sliced
225 g (8 oz) courgettes, thinly sliced
1 green pepper, cored, seeded and chopped
2 cardamom pods, peeled and seeds lightly crushed
1 teaspoon cumin seeds
freshly ground black pepper
2 large tomatoes, skinned and sliced
2 oz mushrooms, sliced
4 tablespoons sultanas
parsley sprigs to garnish

*Preparation time: 25 minutes*
*Cooking time: 25 minutes*

1. Put the millet in a saucepan with the chicken stock and add a little salt. Bring to the boil, stir thoroughly, then cover the pan and simmer for 20 minutes, stirring occasionally, or until the millet is tender and all the stock has been absorbed.
2. Cook the broad beans in boiling, salted water until they are tender. Drain.
3. Heat the oil and fry the onion, courgettes and green pepper over moderate heat for 4-5 minutes, stirring frequently. Stir in the crushed cardamom seeds and the cumin seeds, then season with salt and pepper and cook for 1 minute. Add the tomatoes and mushrooms, stir in well and simmer for 3 minutes.
4. Stir the broad beans and millet into the vegetables, stir in the sultanas and heat gently. Garnish with the parsley sprigs and serve hot.

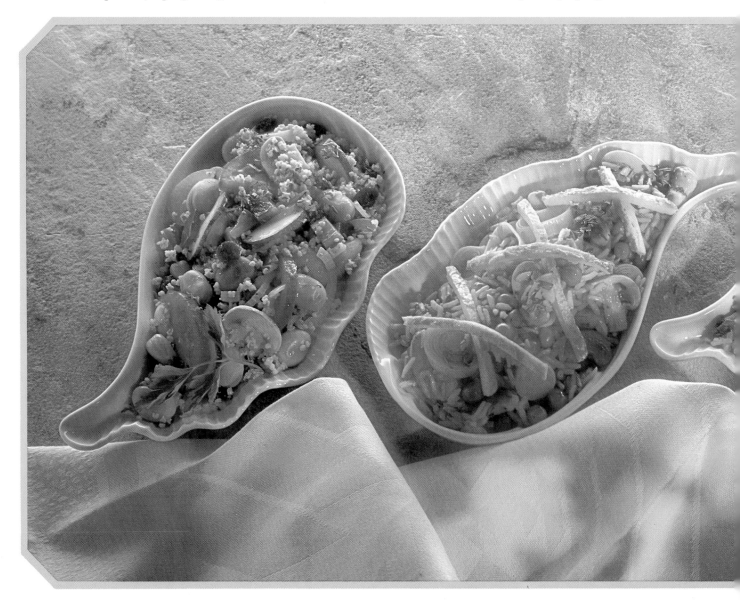

# VEGETABLE FRIED RICE

*Serves 4*

2 large eggs
1 tablespoon water
freshly ground black pepper
15 g (½ oz) butter
2 tablespoons sunflower oil
3 medium leeks, thinly sliced
225 g (8 oz) button mushrooms, thinly sliced
75 g (3 oz) cashew nuts
100 g (4 oz) frozen peas, defrosted
2 tablespoons soy sauce
225 g (8 oz) cooked brown rice, cold
2 tablespoons chopped fresh mint

*Preparation time: 20 minutes*
*Cooking time: 25 minutes*

1. Beat the eggs with the water and season with pepper. Melt the butter in an omelette pan and when it is hot, pour in the egg mixture. Tip the pan to spread the mixture evenly and cook over moderate heat until it is set on one side. Flip the omelette over and cook it to brown the other side. Tip it on to a plate and leave it to cool.
2. Heat the oil in a pan and fry the leeks over moderate heat for 3 minutes, stirring frequently. Add the mushrooms, nuts and peas and stir well. Cook for 1 minute. Stir in the soy sauce and rice and season with pepper. Cook for 5 minutes, stirring frequently.
3. Cut the omelette into thin strips.
4. Stir the mint into the rice and adjust the seasoning if necessary.
5. Turn the rice into a heated serving dish and garnish with the omelette strips arranged in a lattice pattern. Serve hot.

# GREEN RICE

*Serves 4*

225 g (8 oz) brown rice
salt
600 ml (1 pint) chicken stock
4 celery sticks, finely sliced
4 tablespoons chopped celery leaves
225 g (8 oz) spinach leaves, spined and finely
chopped
4 tablespoons chopped fresh parsley
freshly ground black pepper
25 g (1 oz) butter
*To garnish:*
watercress sprigs

*Preparation time: 30 minutes*
*Cooking time: 50 minutes*

1. Put the rice, salt and stock into a pan, stir well and bring to the boil. Cover and simmer gently for 40 minutes.
2. Stir in the sliced celery, the celery leaves, spinach and parsley and season with pepper. Cover the pan and simmer for 5 minutes. Stir in the butter.
3. Turn the rice into a heated serving dish and garnish it with the watercress.

*From the left: Millet and broad bean pilaff; Vegetable fried rice; Green rice.*

## GNOCCHI WITH TOMATO SAUCE

*Serves 4-6*

1 litre (1¾ pints) milk
salt
200 g (7 oz) wholewheat semolina
100 g (4 oz) grated Parmesan cheese
25 g (1 oz) butter
2 egg yolks
¼ teaspoon grated nutmeg
freshly ground black pepper
1 tablespoon chopped fresh oregano,
or parsley, to garnish
*Sauce:*
450 g (1 lb) tomatoes, skinned and chopped
1 tablespoon lemon juice
2 tablespoons tomato purée
1 teaspoon soft light brown sugar
150 ml (¼ pint) sweet cider
1 teaspoon dried oregano

*Preparation time: 30 minutes*
*Cooking time: 45 minutes*
*Oven: 230°C, 450°F, Gas Mark 8*

1. Boil the milk, add salt and gradually stir in the semolina. Simmer very gently for 15 minutes, stirring frequently, until the mixture thickens.
2. Remove from the heat and beat in half the cheese, the butter and the egg yolks.
3. Spread the mixture in a dampened baking tray to a depth of 1 cm (½ inch) and level the top. Leave for at least 1 hour to cool completely.
4. With a 6 cm (2½ inch) biscuit cutter, cut out rounds of the paste and lift them up with a spatula. Arrange them in overlapping circles in a greased, shallow baking dish.
5. Sprinkle the remaining cheese over the dish and sprinkle with the nutmeg.
6. Place in a preheated oven and bake for 20 minutes.
7. To make the sauce, put all the ingredients in a small pan, season well with salt and pepper and bring to the boil. Simmer for 20 minutes, or until the sauce thickens. Beat it thoroughly, taste and adjust the seasoning.
8. Serve the gnocchi garnished with the oregano or parsley, and the sauce separately.

*From the top: Gnocchi with tomato sauce; Spicy dhal.*

## SPICY DHAL

*Serves 4*

225 g (8 oz) yellow split peas, soaked overnight and drained
2 tablespoons sunflower oil
1 large onion, peeled and chopped
2 garlic cloves, peeled and finely chopped
2 teaspoons ground cumin
1 teaspoon ground turmeric
2 spring onions, thinly sliced
2 teaspoons lemon juice
salt
freshly ground black pepper
1 tablespoon chopped fresh coriander leaves, or parsley
*To garnish:*
a few coriander leaves or parsley sprigs
thin spring onions

*Preparation time: 20 minutes, plus overnight soaking*
*Cooking time: 50 minutes*

1. Cook the split peas in boiling, unsalted water for 30-40 minutes, or until they are tender. Drain thoroughly.
2. Heat the oil and fry the onion and garlic over moderate heat for 3 minutes, stirring frequently. Stir in the cumin and turmeric and cook for 3 minutes.
3. Stir in the split peas, spring onions and lemon juice and season with salt and pepper. Cook for a further 2-3 minutes, then taste and adjust the seasoning if necessary. F
4. Turn the mixture into a heated serving dish, sprinkle over the chopped coriander and garnish with spring onions. Serve hot.

F *Freeze for up to 2 months. Thaw at room temperature for 3-4 hours then gently reheat on top of the cooker.*

# VEGETABLES & SALADS

Colourful roots, crisp leafy greens, succulent pods and seeds, flavour-absorbing squashes – vegetables are far too delicious and nutritious to be relegated to the supporting role for they offer an endless and tempting variety as main dishes.

Sadly, all forms of cooking rob vegetables of some of their nutrients and vitamins – especially vitamin C – which disperse in water, heat and on exposure to the air, not only in cooking, but in storage and soaking too. Swish vegetables quickly in water and scrub rather than peel when possible. Potato skins, for example, can be quickly rubbed off after cooking. Steam or simmer in the minimum of water, or bake until only just tender.

Salads must surely be the most nutritious of all fast foods. Choose only the freshest and youngest ingredients and prepare and serve them as soon as possible with the lightest of dressings.

To retain the maximum crispness, toss salad greens in the dressing just before serving. Raw cabbage, celery, mushrooms and peppers may benefit – it's a matter of choice – from being marinated in the dressing for a half-hour or so, and cooked dried beans absorb more flavour if they are coated while still hot in an aromatic dressing.

# VEGETABLE MOUSSAKA

*Serves 4*

100 g (4 oz) brown 'continental' lentils, soaked
overnight and drained
450 g (1 lb) tomatoes, skinned and chopped
1 bay leaf
1 teaspoon dried oregano
1 teaspoon soft dark brown sugar
salt
freshly ground black pepper
sunflower oil, for frying
1 large aubergine, thinly sliced
450 g (1 lb) potatoes, peeled and thinly sliced
*Sauce:*
25 g (1 oz) soft margarine
25 g (1 oz) wholewheat flour
300 ml (½ pint) milk
150 ml (¼ pint) plain unsweetened yogurt
100 g (4 oz) Feta, crumbled, or Wensleydale
cheese, grated
1 egg
large pinch of grated nutmeg

*Preparation time: 30 minutes, plus overnight soaking*
*Cooking time: 2 hours*
*Oven: 190°C, 375°F, Gas Mark 5*

1. Cook the lentils in boiling, unsalted water for 1 hour. Drain.
2. Simmer the tomatoes with the bay leaf, oregano, sugar, salt and pepper for 20 minutes.
3. Stir the lentils into the tomato mixture and simmer for 10 minutes, stirring, until thick.
4. Heat the oil and fry the aubergine slices a few at a time over moderate heat until they begin to colour.
5. Cook the potato slices in boiling, salted water for 10 minutes, or until they begin to soften.
6. Make layers of the tomato and lentil sauce, aubergines and potatoes in a greased casserole, finishing with potatoes.
7. Melt the margarine and stir in the flour. Cook for 1 minute, then remove the pan from the heat. Gradually stir in the milk, then the yogurt. Bring to the boil then simmer for 3 minutes. Remove from the heat. Beat in half of the cheese, and the egg and season with salt, pepper and nutmeg.
8. Pour the sauce over the dish and sprinkle the remaining cheese on top.
9. Stand the casserole on a baking sheet. Place in a preheated oven and bake for 35-40 minutes, or until the sauce is bubbling and browned.

# ASPARAGUS QUICHE

*Serves 6*

175 g (6 oz) wholewheat self-raising flour
salt
50 g (2 oz) white vegetable fat
25 g (1 oz) butter
40 g (1½ oz) cottage cheese, sieved
½-1 teaspoon fennel seeds, lightly crushed
cold water, to mix
*Filling:*
350 g (12 oz) asparagus spears, cooked and
drained
75 g (3 oz) low fat soft cheese
150 ml (¼ pint) plain unsweetened yogurt
6 tablespoons milk
2 eggs
freshly ground black pepper

*Preparation time: 25 minutes, plus chilling*
*Cooking time: 1 hour*
*Oven: 190°C, 375°F, Gas Mark 5*

1. Sift the flour and salt together and tip the bran from the sieve back into the bowl. Rub in the fats until the mixture is like fine breadcrumbs. Stir in the cheese and fennel and mix to a dough with a very little water. Knead the dough lightly. Wrap in clingfilm or foil and chill for at least 30 minutes.
2. Roll out the pastry on a lightly floured board and use to line a greased 20 cm (8 inch) flan ring on a greased baking sheet.
3. Arrange the asparagus spears in a wheel pattern in the pastry case.
4. Mix the cheese, yogurt and milk together, beat in the eggs and season with salt and pepper. Pour the filling into the pastry case.
5. Place in a preheated oven and bake for 40-45 minutes, until the filling is set. F Serve warm.

F *Freeze for up to 2 months. Reheat from frozen in the oven for about 30 minutes.*

*Clockwise from the left: Vegetable moussaka; Fruity aubergine boats; Asparagus quiche.*

# FRUITY AUBERGINE BOATS

*Serves 4*

4 aubergines, about 175 g (6 oz) each
salt
5 tablespoons sunflower oil
1 large onion, peeled and chopped
2 garlic cloves, peeled and finely chopped
450 g (1 lb) tomatoes, skinned and sliced
75 g (3 oz) sultanas
50 g (2 oz) seedless raisins
75 g (3 oz) blanched, slivered almonds
2 tablespoons chopped fresh parsley
½ teaspoon dried thyme
freshly ground black pepper
flat-leaved parsley, to garnish

*Preparation time: 25 minutes*
*Cooking time: 1¼ hours*
*Oven: 180°C, 350°F, Gas Mark 4*

1. Cut off the stalk ends of the aubergines and halve them lengthways. Scoop out the flesh (a curved grapefruit knife is ideal for this), leaving firm 'walls'. Chop the aubergine flesh finely and put it in a colander. Sprinkle liberally with salt and leave for about 1 hour, to degorge (draw off the bitter juices).
2. Rinse the aubergine in cold water and drain thoroughly on kitchen paper.
3. Heat the oil and fry the onion, garlic and aubergine over a moderate heat for 5 minutes, stirring frequently.
4. Add the tomatoes, stir well and fry for a further 5 minutes.
5. Stir in the sultanas, raisins, almonds, parsley and thyme and season with salt and pepper.
6. Stand the aubergine shells cut side up in a greased baking dish and fill them with the tomato mixture.
7. Place in a preheated oven and bake the aubergines for 1 hour. Serve hot, garnished with the parsley leaves.

# CABBAGE BASKET

*Serves 4*

1 small white or green cabbage
salt
450 g (1 lb) carrots
50 g (2 oz) soft margarine
1 medium onion, peeled and chopped
1 garlic clove, peeled and crushed
1 teaspoon ground ginger
1 tablespoon clear honey
100 g (4 oz) cooked brown rice
100 g (4 oz) hazelnuts, chopped
freshly ground black pepper
40 g (1½ oz) fresh wholewheat breadcrumbs
1 hard-boiled egg, finely chopped
1 tablespoon chopped fresh parsley

*Preparation time: 1 hour*
*Cooking time: 1¾ hours*

1. Remove any damaged or discoloured outer leaves from the cabbage and trim to a neat shape. Blanch in boiling, salted water for 5 minutes. Drain thoroughly.
2. Cook the carrots in boiling, salted water for 10 minutes. Drain, reserving the liquid, and chop them finely.
3. Place the cabbage on a board. With 2 large spoons, gently pull a few leaves outwards, to expose the centre leaves and stalk. Remove these, leaving firm 'walls' about 2.5 cm (1 inch) thick. Finely chop the centre leaves.
4. Melt half the margarine and fry the onion and garlic over moderate heat for 3 minutes, stirring once or twice. Stir in the chopped cabbage, carrots, ginger, honey, rice, half the hazelnuts and 4 tablespoons of the reserved carrot stock. Season with salt and pepper, remove from the heat and stir well.
5. Pack the filling into the cabbage 'basket' and wrap it lightly in foil.
6. Stand the cabbage on a trivet in a pan of fast-boiling water, reduce the heat, cover the pan and cook for 1½ hours.
7. Melt the remaining margarine and fry the breadcrumbs and reserved nuts. Stir in the egg and parsley.
8. Transfer the cabbage to a heated serving dish and sprinkle the crumb mixture on top. Serve hot, cut into wedges.

*Clockwise from the left: Cabbage basket; Kitchen-garden loaf; Celery and walnut roll.*

# KITCHEN-GARDEN LOAF

*Serves 6-8*

2 medium carrots, scraped and cut into matchstick strips
175 g (6 oz) asparagus spears
175 g (6 oz) French beans, topped and tailed
salt
25 g (1 oz) soft margarine
1 medium onion, peeled and chopped
1 garlic clove, peeled and crushed
225 g (8 oz) button mushrooms, chopped (reserve 2 for garnish)
225 g (8 oz) cottage cheese
50 g (2 oz) Roquefort cheese, crumbled
4 eggs
150 ml (¼ pint) plain unsweetened yogurt
1 tablespoon chopped fresh parsley
½ teaspoon dried thyme
¼ teaspoon grated nutmeg
freshly ground black pepper
1 hard-boiled egg, sliced, to garnish

over them lengthways along the tin. Pour in one third of the remaining mixture and top with a layer of carrots. Pour on one half of the remaining mixture, top with a layer of beans then pour on the rest of the egg.

6. Stand in a roasting tin half filled with water. Cover with foil. Place in a preheated oven and bake for 1½ hours, or until the egg custard is set. Cool the tin on a wire rack, then chill.
7. Turn the loaf out on to a plate. Garnish with slices of egg and the reserved mushrooms. Leave at room temperature for 30 minutes.
8. To make the dressing, mix all the ingredients together and serve chilled.

## CELERY AND WALNUT ROLL

*Serves 4*

4 eggs, separated
75 g (3 oz) Gruyère cheese, grated
2 teaspoons celery seed
4 tablespoons celery leaves, finely chopped
*Filling:*
175 g (6 oz) low fat soft cheese
75 g (3 oz) walnuts, chopped
2 tablespoons chopped flat-leaved parsley
freshly ground black pepper
celery leaves, to garnish

*Preparation time: 25 minutes*
*Cooking time: 30 minutes*
*Oven: 200° C, 400° F, Gas Mark 6*

1. Line a Swiss roll tin with greased greaseproof paper.
2. Beat the egg yolks until they are creamy, then beat in 25 g (1 oz) of the cheese, celery seed and celery leaves.
3. Whisk the egg whites until stiff and fold them into the celery mixture. Spread the mixture over the prepared tin and level the top.
4. Place in a preheated oven and bake for 25 minutes, or until firm to the touch.
5. Beat together the soft cheese, walnuts and parsley and season with pepper.
6. Remove the tin from the oven. Spread the filling over the sponge base and, using the paper to lift it up, roll it up from one short end.
7. Lift the roll on to a heatproof dish. Sprinkle the remaining cheese on top and return it to the oven for 3-4 minutes to melt the cheese. Serve hot, garnished with celery leaves.

150 ml (¼ p.
1 tea.
½ te
2 tab.
1 t

*Prep*
*C*
*Oven: l*

1. Cook the car... ...oiling, salted water until they are just tender. Drain and plunge at once into cold water to prevent further cooking. Drain again. Pat dry.
2. Grease a 1 kg (2 lb) loaf tin and line it with greased greaseproof paper.
3. Melt the margarine and gently fry the onion and garlic for 3 minutes, stirring. Add the mushrooms and cook for 3 minutes.
4. Blend the onion mixture with the cheese, eggs, yogurt and parsley until smooth. Add the thyme and nutmeg and season.
5. Pour one quarter of the egg and cheese mixture into the prepared tin. Lay the asparagus spears

## SOUFFLÉ COURGETTES

*Serves 4*

6 medium courgettes
salt
350 g (12 oz) tomatoes, skinned and sliced
1 teaspoon dried oregano
freshly ground black pepper
1 tablespoon tomato purée
1 teaspoon lemon juice
2 eggs, separated
1 egg white
75 g (3 oz) Gruyère cheese, grated
pinch of cayenne

*Preparation time: 20 minutes*
*Cooking time: 1 hour*
*Oven: 180°C, 350°F, Gas Mark 4*

1. Cook the courgettes in boiling, salted water for 5 minutes. Drain and cut off the ends. Slice the courgettes in half lengthways and scoop out the flesh, leaving firm 'walls'. Chop the flesh. Leave to cool.
2. Put the tomatoes, oregano, pepper, tomato purée and lemon juice into a pan, stir well and bring to the boil.
3. Beat the egg yolks and chopped courgette flesh together. Whisk the egg whites and fold into the egg yolk mixture with 50 g (2 oz) of the cheese, salt, pepper and cayenne.
4. Spoon the tomato sauce into a baking dish. Arrange the courgette halves on top, cut sides up, and spoon the soufflé mixture into the 'shells'. Sprinkle over the remaining cheese.
5. Place in a preheated oven and bake the courgettes for 35 minutes, or until the cheese mixture is well risen and firm. Serve at once.

*Above: Soufflé courgettes.*
*Right: Vegetable cobbler.*

# VEGETABLE COBBLER

*Serves 6*

3 medium carrots, scraped and thinly sliced
½ small cauliflower, divided into florets
salt
50 g (2 oz) soft margarine
8 small leeks, thickly sliced
2 small heads fennel, sliced
25 g (1 oz) wholewheat flour
450 ml (¼ pint) chicken stock
freshly ground black pepper
2 tablespoons chopped fresh parsley
*Topping:*
175 g (6 oz) wholewheat flour
1 teaspoon bicarbonate of soda
salt
75 g (3 oz) oat flakes
40 g (1½ oz) soft margarine
1 large egg
3 tablespoons plain unsweetened yogurt
50 g (2 oz) Edam cheese, grated

*Preparation time: 45 minutes*
*Cooking time: 1¼ hours*
*Oven: 180°C, 350°F, Gas Mark 4;*
*then: 200°C, 400°F, Gas Mark 6*

1. Cook the carrots and cauliflower in boiling, salted water for 5 minutes. Drain and place in a casserole.
2. Melt half the margarine and fry the leeks and fennel over moderate heat for 4 minutes, stirring frequently. Transfer to the casserole.
3. Melt the remaining margarine, stir in the flour and cook for 1 minute. Remove the pan from the heat and gradually stir in the stock. Season with salt and pepper and bring to the boil. Simmer for 3 minutes. Stir in the parsley and pour the sauce over the vegetables.
4. Cover the casserole and place in a preheated oven for 45 minutes.
5. Sift the flour, soda and salt together and tip the bran from the sieve back into the bowl. Add half the oat flakes and mix in the margarine. Beat in the egg and yogurt to make a firm dough. Shape the dough into a ball and knead lightly until it is smooth.
6. Roll out the dough on a lightly-floured board to 1 cm/½ inch thick and cut into rounds with a biscuit cutter.
7. Arrange the rounds on the vegetables, sprinkle with the cheese mixed with the remaining oat flakes. Increase the oven temperature and bake for 15 minutes, or until the topping is golden. Garnish with fennel fronds. Serve at once.

# PISSALADIÈRE

*Serves 6*

225 g (8 oz) wholewheat flour
salt
100 g (4 oz) soft margarine
1 egg yolk
1 tablespoon plain unsweetened yogurt
1 egg white, lightly beaten
*Filling:*
25 g (1 oz) soft margarine
1 large onion, peeled and finely chopped
2 garlic cloves, peeled and crushed
1 green pepper, cored, seeded and chopped
1 teaspoon mixed dried herbs
freshly ground black pepper
450 g (1 lb) tomatoes, skinned and sliced
50 g (2 oz) Gruyère cheese, grated
40 g (1½ oz) anchovy fillets, drained
black olives, to garnish

*Preparation time: 25 minutes, plus 30 minutes chilling*
*Cooking time: 50 minutes*
*Oven: 200°C, 400°F, Gas Mark 6;*
*then: 180°C, 350°F, Gas Mark 4*

1. Mix the flour and salt together and mix in the margarine, egg and yogurt to form a dough – this method is particularly suitable for a food processor. Lightly knead the dough, wrap in clingfilm or foil and chill in the refrigerator for at least 30 minutes.

2. Melt the margarine and fry the onion, garlic and green pepper over low heat for 10 minutes, stirring frequently. Increase the heat to moderate and fry for a further 2 minutes. Stir in the herbs and season with salt and pepper. Remove from the heat and set aside to cool.

3. Roll out the pastry on a lightly-floured board and use to line 6 greased individual flan dishes or Yorkshire pudding tins. Trim the edges and prick the bases with a fork. Line with grease-proof paper and fill with dried baking beans.

4. Place in a preheated oven and bake 'blind' for 10 minutes. Remove the beans and paper, brush the cases with egg white and return them to the oven for 5 minutes to dry.

5. Spread the onion mixture in the base of each pastry case. Arrange the tomato slices on top. Sprinkle with the cheese and make a lattice with the anchovy fillets. Garnish with the black olives.

6. Reduce the oven temperature and bake for 25 minutes. Serve warm.

# WHOLEWHEAT PIZZA

*Serves 4*

175 g (6 oz) wholewheat self-raising flour
salt
freshly ground black pepper
1 teaspoon dried oregano
50 g (2 oz) soft margarine
6 tablespoons plain unsweetened yogurt
*Filling:*
450 g (1 lb) tomatoes, skinned and sliced
1 teaspoon soft light brown sugar
1 teaspoon dried oregano
1 large onion, peeled and sliced
2 garlic cloves, peeled and crushed
225 g (8 oz) button mushrooms, thinly sliced
1 green pepper, cored, seeded and thinly sliced into rings
1 red pepper, cored, seeded and thinly sliced into rings
100 g (4 oz) Edam cheese, grated
10 black olives, pitted

*Preparation time: 20 minutes*
*Cooking time: 45 minutes*
*Oven: 200°C, 400°F, Gas Mark 6*

1. Mix together the flour, salt, pepper and oregano and mix in the margarine and yogurt. Form the mixture into a ball and knead it lightly until smooth. Roll out the dough on a lightly-floured board and use it to line a 25 cm (10 inch) greased flan ring placed on a greased baking sheet. Line with greaseproof paper and fill with dried baking beans.

2. Place in a preheated oven and bake for 15 minutes.

3. Put the tomatoes, sugar, oregano, onion and garlic into a pan, season with salt and pepper, stir well and bring to the boil. Boil for 20 minutes, stirring once, until the mixture is like a thick sauce. Taste and adjust the seasoning.

4. Spread the tomato mixture over the base of the pizza. Arrange the mushrooms in a single layer and then arrange the pepper rings. Sprinkle the cheese over and garnish with the black olives.

5. Return to the oven and bake for a further 10-15 minutes, or until the cheese is brown and bubbling. Serve hot.

*From the top: Pissaladière; Wholewheat pizza.*

# ONION TART

*Serves 4-6*

25 g (1 oz) soft margarine
2 tablespoons sunflower oil
3 onions, about 750 g (1½ lb), peeled and sliced
3 teaspoons chopped fresh thyme, or 1 teaspoon
dried thyme
1 teaspoon caraway seeds
2 eggs
150 ml (¼ pint) plain unsweetened yogurt
2 tablespoons double cream
freshly ground black pepper
*Pastry:*
175 g (6 oz) wholewheat flour
salt
90 g (3½ oz) vegetable fat or margarine
1 egg yolk
about 2 tablespoons water

*Preparation time: 30 minutes, plus 30 minutes chilling*
*Cooking time: 1 hour*
*Oven: 200°C, 400°F, Gas Mark 6;*
*then: 180°C, 350°F, Gas Mark 4*

1. Melt the margarine with the oil and fry the
   onions over moderately low heat for 20
   minutes, stirring frequently, or until they are
   golden brown. Stir in the thyme and caraway
   seeds and set aside to cool.
2. For the pastry, sift the flour and salt together
   and tip the bran from the sieve back into the
   bowl. Rub in the fat until the mixture is like
   breadcrumbs. Stir in the egg yolk and enough
   water to make a firm dough. Form the dough
   into a ball and knead it lightly until smooth.
   Wrap in clingfilm or foil and chill in the refrigerator for at least 30 minutes.
3. Roll out the dough on a lightly-floured board
   and use to line a greased 20 cm (8 inch) flan
   ring placed on a greased baking sheet. Trim the
   edges and prick the base. Line with a piece of
   greaseproof paper and fill with dried baking
   beans.
4. Place in a preheated oven and bake blind for 10
   minutes. Remove the beans and paper and
   bake the case for a further 5 minutes to dry the
   pastry. Reduce the oven temperature.
5. Beat the eggs, yogurt and cream together and
   season with salt and pepper.
6. Spread the onions over the pastry case and
   pour on the egg mixture.
7. Bake in the oven for 30 minutes, or until the
   filling has set. Serve warm.

# BOREKS

*Serves 4*

225 g (8 oz) potatoes, peeled
2 medium carrots, scraped
4 tablespoons frozen peas
salt
25 g (1 oz) soft margarine
1 small onion, peeled and finely chopped
1 teaspoon wholewheat or wholemeal flour
2 teaspoons ground cumin
½ teaspoon ground ginger
pinch of chilli powder
2 tablespoons chicken stock
1 large tomato, skinned and chopped
freshly ground black pepper
225 g (8 oz) filo pastry
about 4 tablespoons sunflower oil

*Preparation time: 1 hour*
*Cooking time: 40 minutes*
*Oven: 190°C, 375°F, Gas Mark 5*

1. Boil the potatoes, carrots and peas until just tender. Drain. Dice the potatoes and carrots.
2. Melt the margarine and fry the onion over low heat until it is soft. Stir in the flour, cumin, ginger and chilli and pour in the stock. Add the tomato and stir until it forms a paste. Season and stir in the vegetables. Set aside to cool.
3. Unroll the pastry sheets, cut into 23 cm (9 inch) × 10 cm (4 inch) pieces and make 4 piles.
4. Work with a quarter of the pastry at a time and cover the rest with a damp cloth to prevent drying out. Brush the pastry sheets with oil and place each one on top of the other. With the short side of the pastry facing you, place 1 heaped tablespoon of filling 5 cm (2 inches) from the bottom edge. Fold the left corner over the mixture. Continue folding until you have a pastry triangle enclosing the mixture with a 1 cm (½ inch) flap to tuck underneath. Repeat with the remaining pastry and filling.
5. Place the boreks on a greased baking sheet. Place in a preheated oven and bake for 25 minutes or until deep golden brown and crisp.

# STIR-FRIED QUARTET

*Serves 4*

1 small head young celery
225 g (8 oz) broccoli spears
salt
4 spring onions
1 red pepper, cored and seeded
2 tablespoons sunflower oil
5 cm (2 inch) piece fresh root ginger, peeled and cut into very thin strips
4 tablespoons blanched halved almonds
celery leaves, to garnish
*Sauce:*
3 tablespoons dry sherry
1 tablespoon soy sauce
1 teaspoon caster sugar
1 tablespoon clear honey
¾ teaspoon ground ginger
1 tablespoon tomato purée
1 tablespoon cornflour

*Preparation time: 20 minutes*
*Cooking time: 15 minutes*

1. Cut the vegetables into pieces of equal size and shape. Trim the celery, cut off the root end and pull off the stringy outer sticks. Thinly slice the 'heart' diagonally into 1 cm (½ inch) slices. Reserve some of the leaves for garnish. (Use the discarded celery for soup.)
2. Slice the broccoli stems diagonally into 2.5 cm (1 inch) pieces but leave the florets whole and blanch them in boiling, salted water for 2 minutes. Drain.
3. Slice the spring onions diagonally into 5 cm (2 inch) pieces.
4. Core the pepper and cut into thin slices.
5. Mix the sauce ingredients together to make a thin, smooth paste.
6. Heat the oil in a thick, heavy-based frying pan or wok. Stir-fry the celery and ginger over moderately high heat for 3-4 minutes, or until the celery becomes translucent. Add the broccoli, onions and pepper and stir-fry them for 3 minutes.
7. Stir in the sauce and quickly bring to the boil, stirring. Stir-fry for 2 minutes, then add the almonds. Garnish with the celery leaves and serve at once.

*Clockwise from the left: Onion tart; Boreks; Stir-fried quartet.*

# VEGETABLE KEBABS WITH CORIANDER RICE

*Serves 4*

2 medium courgettes
4 button onions or shallots, peeled
salt
8 small button mushrooms, trimmed
4 medium tomatoes, halved, or 8 cherry tomatoes
1 red pepper, cored, seeded and cut into 5 cm
(2 inch) squares
12 small bay leaves
*Marinade:*
4 tablespoons sunflower oil
1 tablespoon red wine vinegar
1 tablespoon lemon juice
1 garlic clove, peeled and crushed
2 tablespoons chopped fresh mint
freshly ground black pepper
½ teaspoon mustard powder
*Rice:*
225 g (8 oz) brown rice
600 ml (1 pint) chicken stock
salt
1 teaspoon ground coriander
2 tablespoons chopped coriander leaves or parsley

*Preparation time: 25 minutes, plus 2 hours marinating*
*Cooking time: 45 minutes*

1.  Blanch the courgettes and onions in boiling, salted water for 2 minutes. Drain.
2.  Trim the courgettes and cut them into 4 cm (1½ inch) slices.
3.  Thread all the vegetables and the bay leaves on to 4 greased skewers and lay them in a shallow dish.
4.  Mix together all the marinade ingredients and pour over the kebabs. Turn in the sauce to coat the vegetables thoroughly. Cover and set aside at room temperature for about 2 hours.
5.  Put the rice in a pan with the stock, salt and ground coriander. Bring to the boil, stir well, cover and simmer for 45 minutes.
6.  Drain the kebabs from the sauce. Place under a preheated moderate grill and cook for 8 minutes, turning frequently and brushing with the remaining marinade.
7.  Stir the chopped coriander into the rice and spoon into a heated serving dish. Arrange the kebabs on top and serve at once. Serve with a green salad.

# MIXED VEGETABLE CURRY

*Serves 4*

1 small cauliflower, cut into florets
225 g (8 oz) carrots, scraped and sliced
225 g (8 oz) French beans, topped, tailed and
sliced
225 g (8 oz) shelled broad beans
175 g (6 oz) frozen sweetcorn
1 large onion, peeled and thinly sliced into rings
salt
50 g (2 oz) raw peanuts
25 g (1 oz) shredded coconut
*Sauce:*
25 g (1 oz) soft margarine
25 g (1 oz) wholewheat or wholemeal flour
2 teaspoons curry powder
1 teaspoon ground turmeric
1 teaspoon ground cumin
300 ml (½ pint) milk
freshly ground black pepper
2 tablespoons double cream

*Preparation time: 25 minutes*
*Cooking time: 25 minutes*

1.  Steam or boil the cauliflower, carrots, beans sweetcorn and onion in salted water until they are just tender. Drain and plunge into cold water to prevent further cooking. Drain again.
2.  For the sauce, melt the margarine and stir in the flour. Cook for 1 minute, then stir in the spices and cook for a further 3 minutes. Gradually stir in the milk, and bring to the boil. Simmer the sauce for 3 minutes. Season with salt and pepper and stir in the cream.
3.  Stir the vegetables and peanuts into the sauce and reheat gently.
4.  Turn the mixture into a heated serving dish and sprinkle with the coconut. Serve hot.

*From the top: Vegetable kebabs with coriander rice; Mixed vegetable curry.*

## ALL THE GREENS

*Serves 4*

1 small curly endive, leaves separated
1 head chicory, leaves torn in half
1 bunch watercress
½ small cucumber, thinly sliced
*Dressing:*
3 tablespoons olive oil
2 teaspoons red wine vinegar
40 g (1½ oz) Roquefort cheese, crumbled
freshly ground black pepper
1 tablespoon plain unsweetened yogurt

*Preparation time: 15 minutes*

*Serve as an accompaniment to a main dish or as a light meal with eggs and crispy rolls.*

1. Toss together all the salad ingredients and put them into a bowl.
2. Mix the dressing.
3. Pour the dressing over the salad just before serving. Toss well.

*Below, from the left: All the greens; Delicatessen delight. Opposite, from the left: Grilled pepper salad; Fennel salad.*

## DELICATESSEN DELIGHT

*Serves 4*

225 g (8 oz) courgettes, thinly sliced diagonally
100 g (4 oz) button mushrooms, thinly sliced
1 small onion, or shallot, peeled and thinly sliced into rings
1 head chicory, leaves separated
100 g (4 oz) smoked salmon, cut into matchstick strips
1 lemon, quartered, to serve
*Dressing:*
3 tablespoons olive oil
1 teaspoon lemon rind
1 tablespoon lemon juice
freshly ground black pepper
a pinch of cayenne
1 tablespoon finely snipped chives

*Preparation time: 30 minutes, plus 30 minutes marinating*

1. Mix the dressing.
2. Toss together the courgettes, mushrooms and onion or shallot. Add the dressing and toss. Leave at room temperature for about 30 minutes.
3. Line a serving dish with the chicory leaves. Spoon the courgette and mushroom salad on top and arrange the smoked salmon strips in the centre. Serve with the lemon wedges.

## GRILLED PEPPER SALAD

*Serves 4*

2 green peppers
1 red pepper
1 yellow pepper (or an extra red pepper)
2 garlic cloves, peeled and finely chopped
2 small onions, peeled and thinly sliced into rings
2 tablespoons chopped parsley
2 tablespoons black olives
1 × 40 g (1½ oz) can anchovy fillets, drained
*Dressing:*
3 tablespoons olive oil
2 teaspoons lemon juice
freshly ground black pepper

*Preparation time: 20 minutes*
*Cooking time: 20 minutes*

1. Place the peppers under a preheated moderately high grill for about 15-20 minutes, turning them frequently, until their skins blacken. Cover with a damp cloth and leave them to cool. Peel.
2. Core and seed the peppers and cut them into thick slices.
3. Toss the peppers with the chopped garlic and the onion rings.
4. Bring the oil and lemon juice just to boiling point. Pour over the peppers and mix well. Leave to cool. Season with pepper.

5. Stir the parsley and olives into the salad. Turn it into a dish and garnish with the anchovy strips.

## FENNEL SALAD

*Serves 4-6*

1 small lettuce heart, shredded
2 medium fennel bulbs, thinly sliced
2 oranges, peeled and thinly sliced into rings
1 bunch watercress
50 g (2 oz) currants
50 g (2 oz) walnut halves
*Dressing:*
3 tablespoons sunflower oil
1 tablespoon orange juice
1 teaspoon orange rind
1 teaspoon red wine vinegar
salt
freshly ground black pepper
1 tablespoon sunflower seeds, crushed

*Preparation time: 25 minutes*

1. Mix the dressing.
2. Toss the lettuce and fennel together.
3. Make a ring of the orange slices around the outside of a dish. Arrange the watercress sprigs in a ring inside them.
4. Just before serving, toss the lettuce and fennel in the dressing and pile the salad in the centre. Make a ring of currants around the green salad. Scatter the walnuts on top.

# SPINACH VINAIGRETTE

*Serves 4*

750 g (1½ lb) young spinach
salt
40 g (1½ oz) pine nuts, or blanched slivered almonds
1 small onion, peeled and thinly sliced into rings
lemon slices, to serve
*Dressing:*
4 tablespoons olive oil
1 tablespoon lemon juice
2 tablespoons chopped mint
freshly ground black pepper
½ teaspoon soft light brown sugar

*Preparation time: 15 minutes*
*Cooking time: 5 minutes*

1. Wash the spinach and cook in the water clinging to the leaves in a large pan for 5 minutes or until tender. Drain in a colander, gently pressing out the water without damaging any of the leaves.
2. Mix all the dressing ingredients together.
3. Mix the spinach in the dressing and stir in the pine nuts. Serve just warm or cool – but not chilled. Garnish with the onion rings, if liked, and serve with lemon slices.

# POTATO AND PARSNIP LAYER

*Serves 6*

450 g (1 lb) potatoes, peeled and cut into 5 mm (¼ inch) slices
1 large onion, peeled and thinly sliced into rings
225 g (8 oz) parsnips, peeled and cut into 5 mm (¼ inch) slices
salt
freshly ground black pepper
pinch of grated nutmeg
300 ml (½ pint) milk or buttermilk
25 g (1 oz) soft margarine

*Preparation time: 20 minutes*
*Cooking time: 2 hours*
*Oven: 180°C, 350°F, Gas Mark 4*

1. Make layers of potato, onion and parsnip in a well-greased baking dish. Dot the potatoes with margarine and season each layer with salt, pepper and nutmeg, finishing with a layer of potatoes. Pour the milk over.
2. Stand the dish on a baking sheet and cover with a lid or foil. Place in a preheated oven and bake for 2 hours. Remove the covering for the last 30 minutes to brown the potatoes. Serve hot.

# ARTICHOKE NESTS

*Serves 4*

750 g (1½ lb) Jerusalem artichokes
1 tablespoon lemon juice
150 ml (¼ pint) chicken stock
25 g (1 oz) soft margarine
4 tablespoons milk
salt
freshly ground black pepper
pinch of grated nutmeg
1 tablespoon chopped fresh mint
1 egg
25 g (1 oz) ground almonds

*Preparation time: 40 minutes*
*Cooking time: 35 minutes*
*Oven: 180°C, 350°F, Gas Mark 4*

1. Peel the artichokes and immediately drop them into a small bowl of water, acidulated with the lemon juice to preserve the colour.
2. Cook the artichokes in the stock for 15 minutes or until tender.
3. Drain and mash them with the margarine, milk, salt, pepper, nutmeg and mint. Beat in the egg and almonds. Beat to make a smooth thick paste. Cool slightly.
4. Using a piping bag and large round nozzle, pipe the artichoke paste on to a greased baking sheet to make 4 round 'nests'.
5. Place in a preheated oven and bake for 20 minutes, or until firm. Fill the nests with cooked vegetables of your choice.

*Clockwise from the top: Spinach vinaigrette; Potato and parsnip layer; Artichoke nests.*

# VEGETABLE STRAWS

*Serves 4*

350 g (12 oz) French beans, topped and tailed, halved if large
350 g (12 oz) carrots, scraped and cut into matchstick strips about 9 cm (3½ inches) long
salt
1 small red pepper, cored, seeded and sliced into rings
1 small green pepper, cored, seeded and sliced into rings
a few Chinese lettuce leaves, shredded
½ bunch watercress
4 tablespoons blanched almonds, toasted
*Dressing:*
4 tablespoons sunflower oil
1 tablespoon red wine vinegar
2 teaspoons orange juice
1 teaspoon orange rind
1 garlic clove, peeled and crushed
½ teaspoon mustard powder
1 tablespoon finely snipped chives
salt
freshly ground black pepper

*Preparation time: 30 minutes*
*Cooking time: 10 minutes*

*Serve with eggs or cheese and wholewheat bread as a light lunch dish, or as part of a salad buffet.*

1.  Cook the beans and carrots separately in boiling, salted water until they are just tender. Drain them, plunge them into cold water and drain again. Blanch the pepper rings in boiling salted water for 1 minute, then drain.
2.  Mix the dressing.
3.  Toss together the Chinese leaves, watercress and almonds. Pile the salad into the centre of a flat serving dish.
4.  Gather up the beans into bundles of 5 or 6 and push each bundle through a red pepper ring.
5.  Make bundles of the carrot sticks and push them through a green pepper ring.
6.  Arrange alternate bunches of beans and carrots around the dish. Pour the dressing over.

*Clockwise from bottom left: Vegetable straws; Italian seafood salad; Spiced mango salad; Applemint bowl.*

# ITALIAN SEAFOOD SALAD

*Serves 4-6*

450 g (1 lb) cooked white fish fillets, such as plaice, skinned and cut into 5 cm (2 inch) slices
100 g (4 oz) peeled prawns
1 × 40 g (1½ oz) can anchovy fillets, drained and chopped
4 tablespoons black olives
2 tablespoons chopped fennel or parsley
salad leaves, to serve
*Dressing:*
3 tablespoons sunflower oil
6 tablespoons dry white wine
1 tablespoon lemon juice
1 small onion or shallot, peeled and chopped
1 garlic clove, peeled and crushed
1 red pepper, cored, seeded and chopped
salt
freshly ground black pepper

*Preparation time: 25 minutes*
*Cooking time: 5 minutes*

*Serve this as a first course or, with the addition of tomato salad, it makes a light lunch or supper dish. It also makes a good dish for summer buffets.*

1. Put all the ingredients for the dressing into a pan and bring to the boil. Leave to cool.
2. Carefully toss together the fish, prawns, anchovies, olives and herb. Pour on the cooled dressing and stir gently, taking care not to break up the fish.
3. Line a dish with the salad leaves. Spoon the salad on top.

## APPLEMINT BOWL

*Serves 4*

3 dessert apples, cored and thinly sliced
75 g (3 oz) raw peanuts
4 celery sticks, thinly sliced
mint and marjoram sprigs, to garnish
*Dressing:*
1 teaspoon lemon rind
2 tablespoons lemon juice
2 tablespoons chopped mint
1 tablespoon chopped marjoram, if available, or parsley
4 tablespoons plain unsweetened yogurt

*Preparation time: 15 minutes*

*Serve with grilled meat or fish dishes. This salad is particularly suitable to accompany pork, herring and mackerel.*

1. Mix the dressing until it is smooth, and have it ready before you slice the apples.
2. Toss together the apples, peanuts and celery and stir in the dressing. Toss to coat the fruit thoroughly. Garnish with the chopped mint and marjoram.

## SPICED MANGO SALAD

*Serves 4*

1 curly endive, leaves separated
3 mangoes, peeled, stoned and thinly sliced
2 dessert apples, cored and chopped
2 teaspoons lemon juice
3 tablespoons pecan nuts
*Dressing:*
1 egg
½ teaspoon Worcestershire sauce
1 tablespoon lemon juice
2 tablespoons plain unsweetened yogurt
salt
freshly ground black pepper

*Preparation time: 20 minutes*

*Serve the salad with cold poultry, game or meat. It is particularly good with rich ingredients such as pork and duck.*

1. Arrange the endive leaves to cover the base of a serving dish.
2. Whisk the egg together with all the other ingredients for the dressing.
3. Toss the mango in the dressing.
4. Toss the apple in the lemon juice and stir in the pecan nuts.
5. Arrange the mango slices in a wheel pattern over the endive and pour on any remaining dressing.
6. Pile the apple and nuts in the centre.

## GRAPEFRUIT SALAD

*Serves 4-6*

3 grapefruit, pink if available, peeled and
segmented
10-12 heads corn salad or 1 bunch watercress
½ small cos lettuce, torn into small pieces
75 g (3 oz) halved almonds, blanched and
toasted
*Dressing:*
3 tablespoons olive oil
2 shallots, peeled and finely chopped
1 tablespoon lemon juice
1 teaspoon clear honey
salt
freshly ground black pepper

*Preparation time: 20 minutes*

*The salad is a tangy accompaniment to grilled poultry, meat and
fish, and makes an interesting starter.*

1. Toss together the grapefruit and corn salad.
Mix the dressing, pour it over the salad and
toss well.
2. Line a serving dish with the lettuce leaves.
3. Just before serving, stir the almonds into the
grapefruit salad and spoon it carefully on to the
bed of lettuce.

## DOMINO SALAD

*Serves 4*

1 small cauliflower, divided into florets
salt
100 g (4 oz) dried chick peas, soaked overnight and
cooked
4 tablespoons black olives
1 bunch watercress
chicory leaves
*Dressing:*
3 tablespoons olive oil
1 tablespoon cider vinegar
1 hard-boiled egg, roughly chopped
1 tablespoon soured cream
salt
freshly ground black pepper

*Preparation time: 20 minutes*
*Cooking time: 10 minutes*

1. Cook the cauliflower in boiling, salted water for
about 8 minutes, until it is barely tender.
Drain, plunge into cold water and drain again.
Leave to cool.
2. Mix the dressing in a blender to emulsify the
ingredients. Check the seasoning.
3. Mix the cauliflower, chick peas, olives and
watercress. Pour on the dressing and toss well.
4. Line a dish with the chicory leaves and arrange
the salad on top.

## FRUIT AND NUT SALAD

*Serves 4-6*

225 g (8 oz) shelled broad beans
salt
1 dessert apple, cored and thinly sliced
2 dessert pears, peeled, cored and thinly sliced
1 tablespoon water
1 tablespoon lemon juice
1 bunch watercress
2 tablespoons macadamia nuts
2 tablespoons walnut halves
1 orange, peeled and segmented
salad leaves, to serve
*Dressing:*
150 ml (¼ pint) plain unsweetened yogurt
2 tablespoons orange juice
1 tablespoon clear honey
2 tablespoons chopped mint
1 spring onion, thinly sliced
salt
freshly ground black pepper

*Preparation time: 20 minutes, plus cooling*
*Cooking time: about 15 minutes*

1. Mix the dressing.
2. Cook the beans in boiling, salted water until
they are just tender. Drain, plunge into cold
water, then drain again and cool.
3. Toss the apple and pear slices in water and
lemon juice as they are cut, then drain them.
4. Mix together the beans, apple and pear slices
and watercress sprigs. Pour on the dressing
and toss so that the salad is well coated. Stir in
the macadamia nuts.
5. Arrange in a serving dish and garnish with the
orange segments.

*Clockwise from top left: Domino salad; Fruit and nut
salad; Grapefruit salad.*

# SPROUTED BEAN SALAD

*Serves 4*

225 g (8 oz) sprouted beans or peas, such as alfalfa,
mung or chick peas
4 spring onions, thinly sliced
½ small cucumber, diced
8 large radishes, thinly sliced
4 tablespoons cashew nuts
2 hard-boiled eggs, quartered
*Dressing:*
150 ml (¼ pint) plain unsweetened yogurt
1 teaspoon clear honey
2 teaspoons soy sauce
1 teaspoon red wine vinegar
1 tablespoon dry sherry
salt
freshly ground black pepper
*Garnish:*
4 spring onions, cut into 'frills'

*Preparation time: 25 minutes, plus 30 minutes soaking*

*This salad can be served as a first course or as a crunchy side dish
with cold meats or fish.*

1. To make spring onion frills, remove the roots from the spring onions and trim to about 7.5 cm (3 inches). Make 6 cuts lengthways through the stalk to within 4 cm (1½ inches) of the end. Soak in iced water for about 30 minutes.
2. Mix the dressing and pour it into 4 individual serving bowls.
3. Toss together the sprouted beans, spring onions, cucumber, radish slices and nuts. Divide the salad between the bowls.
4. Arrange the egg wedges on top of the salad. Garnish each dish with a spring onion frill.

## HI-FI SALAD WITH PEANUT SAUCE

*Serves 6*

225 g (8 oz) young French beans, topped and tailed
salt
2 leeks, thinly sliced
450 g (1 lb) tomatoes, cut into wedges
4 celery sticks, sliced
1 tablespoon sunflower oil
1 teaspoon lemon juice
freshly ground black pepper
1 lemon, quartered, to serve

*Sauce:*
100 g (4 oz) raw peanuts
about 4 tablespoons oil
1 tablespoon red wine vinegar
1 medium onion, peeled and chopped
1 garlic clove, peeled and halved
½ teaspoon chilli powder (or to taste)
sugar

*Preparation time: 30 minutes*
*Cooking time: 15 minutes*

1. Cook the beans in boiling, salted water for 10 minutes, or until they are barely tender. Drain the beans, plunge them into cold water, then drain again. Toss them on crumpled paper towels and set aside to cool.
2. Grease a frying pan with 1 tablespoon of the oil. Fry the peanuts for 5 minutes over moderate heat, stirring frequently. Leave the nuts to cool.
3. Grind the nuts in a blender with the remaining three tablespoons of oil, the vinegar, onion, garlic, chilli powder and sugar.
4. Toss together the beans, leeks, tomatoes and celery. Pour on the oil and lemon juice and season with pepper. Toss well.
5. Serve the salad with the lemon wedges, and the sauce separately.

*Opposite: Sprouted bean salad.*
*Below: Hi-fi salad with peanut sauce.*

# WEST INDIAN CHICKEN SALAD

*Serves 6*

4 celery sticks, thinly sliced
4 slices fresh pineapple, cubed
50 g (2 oz) pecan nuts
1.1 kg (2½ lb) cooked chicken, skinned, boned and sliced
1 small lettuce heart, shredded
1 avocado, halved, stoned, peeled and sliced
1 tablespoon lemon juice
*Dressing:*
150 ml (¼ pint) plain unsweetened yogurt
1 teaspoon curry powder
1 teaspoon curry paste
1 tablespoon double cream
1 teaspoon clear honey
½ teaspoon lemon juice
salt
freshly ground black pepper

*Preparation time: 35 minutes*

*Serve as a main course, with a tomato salad and slices of wholewheat bread.*

*1.* Mix the dressing.
*2.* Toss together the celery, pineapple and pecans and pour on the dressing. Stir to mix well. Add the chicken and toss carefully to avoid breaking up the meat.
*3.* Arrange the lettuce in a ring around the outside of a serving dish. Toss the avocado slices in lemon juice as soon as they are cut. Arrange them over the lettuce.
*4.* Spoon the chicken salad into the centre of the serving dish.

# ROMAN SALAD

*Serves 4*

225 g (8 oz) shelled broad beans
salt
225 g (8 oz) young spinach leaves, finely shredded
100 g (4 oz) button mushrooms, thinly sliced
3 large firm tomatoes, skinned, seeded and chopped
a few sprigs of fennel leaves, if available, or parsley

*Dressing:*
3 tablespoons olive oil
1 tablespoon cider vinegar
freshly ground black pepper
1 tablespoon clear honey
½ teaspoon mustard powder
50 g (2 oz) Mozzarella cheese, cubed

*Preparation time: 15 minutes*
*Cooking time: about 15 minutes*

*1.* Cook the beans in boiling, salted water until they are just tender. Drain, plunge at once into cold water and drain again. Leave to cool.
*2.* Mix the dressing.
*3.* Toss together the beans, spinach, mushrooms and tomatoes. Just before serving, pour on the dressing and toss well. Garnish with the fennel leaves or other herb sprigs.

# SWEET CABBAGE SALAD

*Serves 4*

350 g (12 oz) white cabbage, shredded
100 g (4 oz) button mushrooms, sliced
6 tablespoons sultanas
4 tablespoons pumpkin seeds
4 tablespoons cashew nuts
*Dressing:*
2 tablespoons clear honey
1 tablespoon lemon juice
1 teaspoon lemon rind
1 teaspoon cider vinegar
salt
pepper
3 tablespoons plain unsweetened yogurt
spring onions, to garnish

*Preparation time: 20 minutes, plus 30 minutes marinating*

*Serve as part of a cold buffet or to accompany grilled or cold poultry and meats.*

*1.* Mix the dressing.
*2.* Toss together the cabbage, mushrooms and sultanas. Pour on the dressing, toss well and leave at room temperature for about 30 minutes.
*3.* Stir in the pumpkin seeds and nuts.
*4.* Garnish with spring onions.

*Clockwise from the left: Sweet cabbage salad; Roman salad; West Indian chicken salad.*

## GREEK ISLAND SALAD

*Serves 4-6*

1 small cos lettuce, thinly sliced
½ small cucumber, thinly sliced
2 green peppers, cored, seeded and thinly sliced
1 large onion, peeled and thinly sliced into rings
3 large tomatoes, thinly sliced into rings
100 g (4 oz) Feta cheese, thinly sliced
salt
freshly ground black pepper
about 4 tablespoons olive oil
2 teaspoons chopped dill, or parsley
sprig dill or parsley, to garnish

*Preparation time: 20 minutes*

*Serve as an accompaniment to main fish or meat dishes.*

*1.* Arrange the salad in layers, in a glass bowl if possible, in the order in which the ingredients are listed, seasoning each layer with a little salt.

*2.* Pour half the oil over the tomato layer. Arrange the cheese on top and pour on the remaining oil. Sprinkle on the herb and garnish with a separate sprig.

## APPLE TREE SALAD

*Serves 4-6*

2 dessert apples, cored and thinly sliced
2 teaspoons lemon juice
225 g (8 oz) button mushrooms, thinly sliced
225 g (8 oz) black grapes, halved and seeded
2 medium carrots, scraped and grated
2 tablespoons roasted sesame seeds
*Dressing:*
2 tablespoons olive oil
1 tablespoon cloudy apple juice
2 tablespoons soured cream
salt
freshly ground black pepper

*Preparation time: 25 minutes*

*This salad is equally good served as a starter or as an accompaniment to cold main dishes.*

1. Mix the dressing ingredients until they are well blended.
2. Toss the apples in the lemon juice. Reserve a few apple and mushroom slices to garnish. Mix together the remaining apple and mushroom slices, the grapes, carrots and sesame seeds.
3. Pour on the dressing and mix well. Garnish the salad with the reserved apple and mushroom slices.

# HIGHLAND POTATOES

*Serves 4*

450 g (1 lb) small potatoes
salt
2 large eggs, beaten
1 tablespoon milk
freshly ground black pepper
5 tablespoons rolled oats
1 tablespoon wholewheat flour
sunflower oil, for deep-frying
watercress sprigs, to garnish (optional)

*Preparation time: 20 minutes*
*Cooking time: about 20 minutes*

1. Partly cook the potatoes in boiling, salted water for 12-15 minutes. Drain and leave them for about 10 minutes to cool.
2. Beat the egg and milk together and season with salt and pepper. Roll the potatoes in the egg to coat them on all sides.
3. Mix together the oats and flour. Roll or toss the potatoes in this mixture then roll again in the egg and toss once more in the mixture until they are well covered.
4. Heat the oil for deep frying to 180°-190°C/ 350°-375°F or until a cube of bread browns in 30 seconds. Deep-fry the potatoes in batches for about 3-4 minutes or until golden brown. Drain on kitchen paper.
5. Serve hot. Garnish with watercress sprigs if liked.

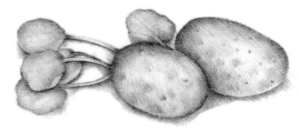

*From the left: Greek island salad; Apple tree salad; Highland potatoes.*

# DESSERTS

There's a new style to the desserts that constitute the final flourish to a wholefood menu. Many of them bear a marked resemblance to old favourites and are reassuringly familiar, though lower in both calories and cholesterol. All the delightful and appetizing combinations of fresh fruits – cherries, peaches, plums, apricots, raspberries, strawberries, apples, melons – are there; but the dressing is likely to be devised from unsweetened fruit juices (containing natural fruit sugars) rather than a sugar-and-water syrup. There's ice cream to tingle the palate on a hot day; but the base is likely to be fruit purée rather than custard, and blended with yogurt in place of cream. And there are steamed and baked puddings to bring a glow in winter and draw attention once again to the versatility of wholegrain flours. Our Christmas pudding recipe omits the traditional animal fat – suet – and so is suitable for vegetarians. It is also ideal for everyone who wants to cut down on their cholesterol intake.

Yogurt is indispensable as a cream substitute in low-calorie wholefood cooking; the new 'thick and creamy' kinds and the Greek cow's milk yogurt now so much more readily available make the healthy subterfuge almost impossible to detect.

# BLACKCURRANT SESAME CRUMBLE

*Serves 4-6*

225 g (8 oz) cooking apples, peeled, cored and
thinly sliced
350 g (12 oz) blackcurrants, stripped from stalks
2 tablespoons water
40 g (1½ oz) soft light brown sugar
*Topping:*
150 g (5 oz) wholewheat flour
75 g (3 oz) hard margarine
25 g (1 oz) toasted sesame seeds
40 g (1½ oz) demerara sugar
1 teaspoon ground cinnamon

*Preparation time: 20 minutes*
*Cooking time: 50 minutes*
*Oven: 160°C, 325°F, Gas Mark 3*

*Plain yogurt or soured cream go well with this pudding.*

1. Simmer the apples and blackcurrants with the water for 5 minutes. Stir in the sugar. Turn the mixture into a shallow baking dish.
2. Rub together the flour and margarine until the mixture is like fine crumbs, then stir in the sesame seeds, sugar and cinnamon.
3. Sprinkle the topping over the fruit and level the top. **F**
4. Stand the dish on a baking sheet. Bake in a preheated oven for 40-45 minutes, or until the topping is golden brown. Serve hot or warm.

**F** *You can freeze the uncooked pudding for up to 2 months. Bake it from frozen, in the oven at 190°C, 375°F, Gas Mark 5 for 45-50 minutes.*

# APPLE SORBET

*Serves 4*

150 ml (¼ pint) dry white wine
50 g (2 oz) soft light brown sugar
a strip of thinly-pared lemon rind
2 tablespoons lemon juice
a piece of fresh root ginger, peeled
450 g (1 lb) cooking apples, peeled, cored and
sliced
small angelica or other herb leaves, to decorate

*Preparation time: 15 minutes, plus 4-5 hours freezing*
*Cooking time: 15 minutes*

1. Put the wine, sugar, lemon rind, lemon juice and ginger into a pan and stir over a low heat until the sugar has dissolved. Increase the heat and bring to the boil.

2. Add the apple slices and poach them for 8-10 minutes, or until they are tender. Remove from the heat and leave to cool.

3. Discard the lemon rind and ginger and liquidize the fruit and juice in a blender.

4. Pour the mixture into a container, cover with foil and freeze for 1 hour.

5. Turn the mixture into a chilled bowl and beat it to break down the ice crystals.

6. Return the mixture to the freezer for 3-4 hours, until it is firm. ☒

7. To serve, transfer the sorbet to the refrigerator for about 30 minutes. Serve it in scoops, decorated with the herb leaves.

☒ *You can store the sorbet for up to 2 months without loss of flavour.*

*Clockwise from the left: Apple sorbet; Blackcurrant sesame crumble; Greengage brandy snap cups.*

# GREENGAGE BRANDY SNAP CUPS

*Serves 6*

50 g (2 oz) wholewheat flour
½ teaspoon ground ginger
50 g (2 oz) soft light brown sugar
2 tablespoons clear honey
50 g (2 oz) soft margarine
½ teaspoon lemon rind
1 teaspoon lemon juice
*Filling:*
450 g (1 lb) greengages, stoned
2 tablespoons water
3 tablespoons clear honey
300 ml (½ pint) plain unsweetened yogurt
scented geranium leaves, to decorate
1 orange, for making the cups

*Preparation time: 45 minutes*
*Cooking time: 40 minutes*
*Oven: 190°C, 375°F, Gas Mark 5*

1. Mix together the flour and ginger. Heat the sugar, honey and margarine over a low heat and stir together until the ingredients are well blended. Remove the pan from the heat, tip in the flour and beat well. Beat in the lemon rind and lemon juice.

2. Line a baking tray with non-stick silicone paper. Drop teaspoonfuls of the mixture on to the baking tray, leaving plenty of space between them.

3. Bake in a preheated oven for 8-10 minutes. Remove the brandy snaps one at a time and – working very quickly, before they harden – press each one over an orange held in the palm of your hand to form the cups. Place the brandy snap cups upside down on a wire rack to cool. When they are completely cold, they can be stored in an airtight tin.

4. To make the filling, reserve 3 greengages to decorate and simmer the remainder in the water and honey syrup. When the greengages are soft, press them through a sieve. Return the purée to the pan and simmer until it is thick. Set aside to cool.

5. Beat together the cooled purée and the yogurt.

6. Just before serving, fill the cups with the purée. Cut the reserved greengages into thin slices and arrange a few on each cup to form a flower shape. Arrange scented geranium leaves in the centre to decorate.

## BROWN SUGAR MERINGUES WITH BRAMBLE SAUCE

*Serves 4*

2 egg whites
2 drops lemon juice
100 g (4 oz) soft light brown sugar
1 teaspoon cornflour
½ teaspoon vanilla essence
*Sauce:*
2 cooking apples, peeled, cored and chopped
150 ml (¼ pint) sweet cider
350 g (12 oz) blackberries
2 tablespoons cassis sirop (optional)
*Filling:*
225 g (8 oz) low fat soft cheese

*Preparation time: 45 minutes*
*Cooking time: 2¾ hours*
*Oven: 110°C, 225°F, Gas Mark ¼*

1. Whisk the egg whites with the lemon juice until they are stiff and stand in peaks. Add half the sugar and whisk until the mixture is stiff and glossy. Fold in the remaining sugar with the cornflour and vanilla essence.

2. Line 2 baking trays with non-stick silicone paper. Using a piping bag and medium star nozzle, pipe 8 thick S shapes and 8 swirls of meringue on to the paper.

3. Bake in the oven for 1½ hours, changing the trays from higher to lower shelves after 45 minutes, until firm on the surface.

4. Peel the meringues from the paper and place them upside down on the trays.

5. Return the meringues to the oven for 1 hour to dry completely.

6. Cool the meringues on a wire rack. When they are cold, store them in an airtight tin.

7. Simmer the apples in the cider until they are tender. Liquidize them in a blender. Return to the pan, add the blackberries and sirop, if using. Simmer for 5 minutes. Serve hot or cold.

8. Just before serving, sandwich the meringues together in pairs with the cheese. Serve the sauce separately.

*Below: Brown sugar meringues with bramble sauce.*
*Opposite, from the top: Strawberry wine syllabub; Frozen cranberry cheese.*

1. Melt the honey in the water. Add the cranberries and simmer them for 10 minutes, or until they are tender. Leave to cool.
2. Liquidize the fruit in a blender and rub it through a sieve.
3. Beat together the cheese and soured cream. Gradually beat in the fruit purée, the syrup and orange juice. Beat until the mixture is smooth – or use a blender or food processor.
4. Turn the mixture into a decorative 900 ml (1½ pint) mould. Cover with foil and freeze for 4 hours.
5. To make the sauce, melt the honey in the water and orange juice. Add the cranberries and simmer for 5 minutes. Do not allow them to break up. Pour a little of the juice into the cornflour and mix to make a smooth paste. Add the mixture to the fruit and stir gently over a low heat for 4-5 minutes until the sauce thickens and becomes transparent. Cool.
6. Unmould the dessert and leave it in the refrigerator for 1¼ hours to soften. Decorate with mint leaves. Serve the sauce separately.

## FROZEN CRANBERRY CHEESE

*Serves 6*

75 g (3 oz) thick honey
2 tablespoons water
175 g (6 oz) fresh or frozen cranberries
350 g (12 oz) low fat soft cheese
150 ml (¼ pint) soured cream
3 tablespoons grenadine or rosehip syrup
1 tablespoon orange juice
mint leaves, to decorate
*Sauce:*
2 tablespoons thick honey
2 tablespoons water
2 tablespoons orange juice
175 g (6 oz) fresh or frozen cranberries
1 teaspoon cornflour

*Preparation time: 30 minutes, plus 4 hours freezing*
*Cooking time: 25 minutes*

*This is a lovely 'alternative Christmas pudding' to make when fresh cranberries are in season – though frozen ones are good too.*

## STRAWBERRY WINE SYLLABUB

*Serves 6*

300 ml (½ pint) plain unsweetened yogurt, Greek if available
2 teaspoons orange rind
1 tablespoon orange juice
50 g (2 oz) soft light brown sugar
100 ml (3½ fl oz) rosé wine
450 g (1 lb) strawberries, halved if large

*Preparation time: 20 minutes, plus 1 hour chilling*

*This dessert is best made shortly before serving. If it is left for more than an hour or so, the wine may separate and sink to the bottom. But it's still delicious!*

1. Beat the yogurt with the orange rind and orange juice. Beat in the sugar, then gradually pour on the wine, beating all the time. Chill in the refrigerator for at least 1 hour.
2. Reserve a few of the best strawberries to decorate. Lightly stir the remainder into the syllabub.
3. Pour the dessert into a bowl or 6 individual glasses and decorate with the reserved strawberries.

## ICED GINGER MERINGUE

*Serves 6-8*

2 egg whites
90 g (3½ oz) soft light brown sugar
½ teaspoon ground ginger
300 ml (½ pint) plain unsweetened yogurt,
Greek if available
4 tablespoons double cream
2 teaspoons lemon rind
2 teaspoons lemon juice
*Sauce:*
350 g (12 oz) raspberries
2 tablespoons lemon juice
2 tablespoons clear honey

*Preparation time: 40 minutes, plus about 3 hours freezing*
*Cooking time: 3 hours*
*Oven: 110°C, 225°F, Gas Mark ¼*

1. Whisk the egg whites until they are stiff, then whisk in half the sugar until the mixture is stiff and glossy. Mix the remaining sugar with the ground ginger and fold into the egg whites.
2. Line a baking sheet with non-stick silicone paper and spoon on mounds of the mixture.
3. Bake the meringues in a preheated oven for 2½-3 hours, until they are dry.
4. Cool the meringues on a wire rack. Peel them from the paper and leave them to become completely cold. **A**
5. Whip together the yogurt and cream and beat in the lemon rind and lemon juice. Crush the meringues into chunks and stir them into the mixture.
6. Line a 450 g (1 lb) loaf tin with foil and turn the mixture into it. Cover with foil and freeze for about 3 hours. There is no need to stir the mixture again.
7. Sieve the raspberries and stir in the lemon juice and honey.
8. Turn out the meringue 'loaf' on to a serving dish and leave it in the refrigerator for 30 minutes before serving.
9. Dribble a little of the sauce over it to decorate and serve the rest separately.

**A** *You can make the brown sugar meringues well in advance and store them in an airtight tin.*

*Clockwise from the left: Iced ginger meringue; Set-alight salad; Honeyed Greek yogurt.*

## HONEYED GREEK YOGURT

*Serves 4*

600 ml (1 pint) Greek plain unsweetened yogurt
2 tablespoons sweet sherry
3 tablespoons clear honey
1 tablespoon soft dark brown sugar
8 fresh figs, quartered

*Preparation time: 15 minutes, plus 2 hours chilling*

1. Beat the yogurt, sherry and honey. Decorate with sugar, cover and chill for at least 2 hours.

*2.* Just before serving, cut the fresh figs into quarters and serve with the yogurt.

# SET-ALIGHT SALAD

*Serves 6*

150 ml (¼ pint) red grape juice
2 tablespoons water
1 tablespoon lemon juice
2 bay leaves
450 g (1 lb) redcurrants, stripped from stalks
225 g (8 oz) gooseberries, topped and tailed
225 g (8 oz) raspberries
2 tablespoons brandy

*Preparation time: 30 minutes*
*Cooking time: 10 minutes*

*1.* Bring the grape juice, water, lemon juice and bay leaves to the boil in a large pan and simmer for 3 minutes. Ⓐ

*2.* Add the redcurrants and gooseberries and bring to the boil in the syrup. Simmer for 3-4 minutes. Add the raspberries and just return to the boil. Transfer the fruit and syrup to a serving dish.

*3.* Pour the brandy into a warmed ladle and set light to it. Pour the flaming brandy on to the fruit. Serve at once.

Ⓐ *You can prepare the syrup in advance, then quickly reheat it when you have prepared all the fruit and are ready to serve the dessert.*

## PEAR CLAFOUTI

*Serves 4*

40 g (1½ oz) wholewheat flour
salt
40 g (1½ oz) soft light brown sugar
2 eggs
1 egg yolk
1 tablespoon sunflower oil
300 ml (½ pint) milk
450 g (1 lb) dessert pears, such as Conference,
peeled, cored and sliced
1 tablespoon lemon juice
2 tablespoons demerara sugar

*Preparation time: 20 minutes*
*Cooking time: 45 minutes*
*Oven: 180°C, 350°F, Gas Mark 4*

1. Mix together the flour, a pinch of salt and the sugar. Beat in the eggs, the egg yolk and the oil. Gradually pour on the milk, beating constantly.
2. Toss the pears in the lemon juice and arrange them in a greased, shallow baking dish. Pour on the batter.
3. Bake the pudding in a preheated oven for 30 minutes. Dust with the demerara sugar and bake for a further 10-15 minutes. Serve hot.

## GINGERED FRUITS

*Serves 6*

450 g (1 lb) mixed dried fruits – apple rings,
apricots, peaches, pears, prunes, soaked overnight
in 600 ml (1 pint) water
1 piece fresh root ginger, peeled and halved
4 tablespoons ginger wine
2 teaspoons lemon juice
2 dessert apples, cored and thinly sliced
2 tablespoons blanched almonds, toasted
*Sauce:*
250 ml (8 fl oz) plain unsweetened yogurt
2 pieces preserved ginger, finely chopped
1 tablespoon ginger syrup
1 teaspoon lemon juice

*Preparation time: 10 minutes, plus overnight soaking*
*Cooking time: 30 minutes*

*Clockwise from the top: Gingered fruits; Plum soufflé; Pear clafouti.*

1. Put the fruits in a pan with the remaining soaking water, the pieces of ginger, ginger wine and lemon juice and bring slowly to the boil. Simmer for 25 minutes, or until the fruits are tender. Leave to cool.
2. Remove the ginger. Stir in the apple slices and, just before serving, the toasted almonds.
3. Mix together the yogurt, chopped ginger, syrup and lemon juice.
4. Serve the fruits cold but not chilled, with the sauce separately.

## PLUM SOUFFLÉ

*Serves 4*

450 g (1 lb) dessert plums, stoned
2 teaspoons lemon juice
2 tablespoons water
2 tablespoons wholewheat semolina
2 tablespoons ground almonds
2 eggs, separated
2 tablespoons Amaretto liqueur (optional)
4 tablespoons blanched flaked almonds,
toasted

*Preparation time: 40 minutes*
*Cooking time: 45 minutes*
*Oven: 190°C, 375°F, Gas Mark 5*

1. Simmer the plums with the lemon juice and water until they are tender. Press them through a sieve. Return the purée to the pan and stir in the semolina. Bring to the boil and simmer for 10 minutes. Cool.
2. Beat the ground almonds into the cooled purée. Beat in the egg yolks and liqueur.
3. Whisk the egg whites until they are stiff. Fold them into the fruit mixture.
4. Spoon the mixture into 4 greased individual soufflé dishes. Stand them in a roasting pan with water to come half way up the sides.
5. Bake the soufflés in a preheated oven for 20 minutes, or until the mixture is just set.
6. Scatter the almonds on top and serve at once.

# MINT ICE FOLDS

*Serves 4*

75 g (3 oz) soft light brown sugar
150 ml (¼ pint) water
50 g (2 oz) mint leaves
2 tablespoons lemon juice
300 ml (½ pint) plain unsweetened yogurt
*Sauce:*
2 medium cooking apples, peeled, cored and
chopped
2 tablespoons water
3 tablespoons crème de menthe liqueur
2 tablespoons clear honey
1 tablespoon lemon juice
*To garnish:*
mint sprigs

*Preparation time: 30 minutes, plus 4-5 hours freezing*
*Cooking time: 20 minutes*

1. Put the sugar and water into a pan and stir over low heat to dissolve the sugar. Add the mint leaves, bring to the boil and simmer for 5 minutes. Remove from the heat and leave to become completely cold.
2. Strain off the mint leaves, pressing them against the sieve to extract all the moisture and flavour.
3. Stir the lemon juice into the cold syrup. Pour it into the yogurt, beating constantly.
4. Pour the mixture into a container, cover with foil and freeze for 1 hour.
5. Turn the partly frozen mixture into a chilled bowl and beat it thoroughly to break down the ice crystals.
6. Return the mixture to the freezer for 3-4 hours, until it is firm.
7. To make the sauce, simmer the apples in the water until they are mushy. Beat them well or liquidize them in a blender, then stir in the liqueur, honey and lemon juice. Simmer for 3-4 minutes, stirring frequently. Leave to cool.
8. Transfer the pudding to the refrigerator for 30 minutes. Scoop it from the container with a tablespoon and arrange the 'folds' on a dish. Decorate with the mint sprigs. Serve the sauce separately.

*Clockwise from the left: Mint ice folds; Corinth pancakes;*
*Red fruit salad.*

# RED FRUIT SALAD

*Serves 4*

750 g (1½ lb) raspberries
4 tablespoons clear honey
225 g (8 oz) dessert cherries, pitted
225 g (8 oz) blackcurrants, stripped from stalks
*Curd cheese:*
2 teaspoons gelatine crystals
2 tablespoons hot water
350 g (12 oz) cottage cheese, sieved
150 ml (¼ pint) plain unsweetened yogurt
4 tablespoons double cream
grated nutmeg

*Preparation time: 30 minutes, plus overnight draining*
*Cooking time: 5 minutes*

1. Sprinkle the gelatine on the water in a small bowl. Stir well and stand the bowl in hot water

to dissolve the crystals.

2. Beat together the cottage cheese, the yogurt and the cream, then stir in the dissolved gelatine.

3. Spoon the mixture into 4 draining moulds or yogurt pots. To use yogurt pots, cover them with muslin and invert them to drain over a dish. Leave overnight.

4. Liquidize half the raspberries, then sieve them. Stir the honey into the purée over a low heat. Stir in the remaining raspberries, the cherries and blackcurrants and simmer for 2-3 minutes. Cool, then chill in the refrigerator for at least 1 hour. Ⓕ

5. Turn out the curd cheese moulds and decorate them with a pinch of grated nutmeg. Serve them with the fruit salad as a substantial 'sauce'.

Ⓕ *The fruit salad can be frozen, but not the curd cheese moulds.*

# CORINTH PANCAKES

*Makes 8 pancakes*

100 g (4 oz) wholewheat flour
salt
1 egg, beaten
150 ml (¼ pint) unsweetened orange juice
150 ml (¼ pint) soda water
oil or fat, for frying
demerara sugar, for sprinkling
*Filling:*
225 g (8 oz) low fat soft cheese
150 ml (¼ pint) plain unsweetened yogurt
1 tablespoon lemon rind
2 teaspoons lemon juice
100 g (4 oz) currants
50 g (2 oz) dried stoned dates, chopped

*Preparation time: 20 minutes*
*Cooking time: 45 minutes*

1. Mix together the flour and salt and beat in the egg. Gradually beat in the orange juice and soda water.

2. Use the minimum of oil or fat to grease a 20 cm (8 inch) omelette pan. When the pan is hot, pour in enough of the batter to cover the base with a thin film. Cook until the pancake is brown and bubbling on the underside. Flip or toss and cook the other side.

3. Keep the cooked pancakes warm while you make the remainder of the batch.

4. Beat together the cheese, yogurt, lemon rind and lemon juice. Stir in the currants and dates.

5. Spread the mixture over each pancake. Fold each one in half, then in half again, so that they are wedge-shaped.

6. Arrange the pancakes in a heated flameproof dish. Sprinkle on the demerara sugar and cook them under a preheated moderate grill for 3-4 minutes until the sugar caramelizes.

# CHRISTMAS PUDDING

*Serves 12*

225 g (8 oz) soft margarine
2 eggs, beaten
100 g (4 oz) wholewheat flour
100 g (4 oz) fresh wholewheat breadcrumbs
1 teaspoon mixed ground spice
1 teaspoon ground cinnamon
½ teaspoon ground nutmeg
225 g (8 oz) seedless raisins
225 g (8 oz) currants
100 g (4 oz) sultanas
225 g (8 oz) dried stoned dates, chopped
50 g (2 oz) dried figs, chopped
50 g (2 oz) blanched chopped almonds
50 g (2 oz) hazelnuts, chopped
3 tablespoons molasses
2 tablespoons orange rind
4 tablespoons orange juice
150 ml (¼ pint) milk
4 tablespoons brandy

*Preparation time: 1¼ hours*
*Cooking time: 4 hours*

1. Beat the margarine and gradually beat in the eggs. In a separate bowl, mix together the flour, breadcrumbs and spices and stir them into the egg mixture. Stir in all the remaining ingredients. Beat well until all the liquid has been evenly incorporated.
2. Divide the mixture between 2 greased 900 ml (1½ pint) pudding basins. Cover them with a piece of greased greaseproof paper and foil, pleated along the centre to allow for rising.
3. Place the basins on a trivet in 2 pans and pour in fast-boiling water to come half-way up the sides. Cover the pans and steam for 4 hours, topping up with more boiling water as needed.
4. Lift out the puddings and cool them on a wire rack. Replace the covers with fresh, greased greaseproof paper and foil. When they are completely cold, store them in a cool dry place for up to 1 year.
5. To reheat the puddings, steam them in a covered pan of fast-boiling water for 2½ hours.

*Above: Christmas pudding.*
*Opposite, from the left: Plum brûlée; Nomad pudding.*

## PLUM BRÛLÉE

*Serves 6*

750 g (1½ lb) Victoria plums
2 tablespoons soft light brown sugar
*Topping:*
450 ml (¾ pint) plain unsweetened yogurt, Greek
if available
150 ml (¼ pint) soured cream
50 g (2 oz) soft light brown sugar

*Preparation time: 20 minutes, plus several hours chilling*
*Cooking time: 10 minutes*

1. Blanch the plums in boiling water for 2 minutes. Drain them.
2. Halve and stone the plums and arrange them, cut sides down, in a flameproof dish. Sprinkle on the sugar.
3. Beat together the yogurt and soured cream.
4. Spread the yogurt mixture over the fruit, cover and chill in the refrigerator for several hours, or overnight.
5. About 2 hours before serving, sprinkle the sugar evenly over the yogurt topping.
6. Place under a preheated medium hot grill and cook for 5 minutes, or until the sugar topping has caramelized. Cool, then chill.

## NOMAD PUDDING

*Serves 6*

600 ml (1 pint) milk
40 g (1½ oz) wholewheat semolina
25 g (1 oz) soft light brown sugar
2 eggs, beaten
2 teaspoons rosewater
50 g (2 oz) ground almonds
rose petals, to decorate
25 g (1 oz) pistachio nuts, chopped, to decorate

*Preparation time: 10 minutes*
*Cooking time: 30 minutes*

1. Put the milk in a pan and sprinkle on the semolina, stirring constantly. Add the sugar and bring to the boil, still stirring.
2. Simmer for 15 minutes, until the mixture has thickened.
3. Remove the pan from the heat, cool slightly and beat in the eggs, rosewater and almonds. Return to the heat and simmer very gently for 10 minutes.
4. Pour the mixture into 6 small greased individual dishes. Leave them to cool.
5. Decorate the puddings with the rose leaves and sprinkle with chopped nuts. Serve cold but not chilled.

# BAKING

Wholefood baking really means turning back the clock – shades of huge farm kitchens, roaring fires, a griddle iron over the ashes – and appreciating once again good wholesome *whole* ingredients. It means using whole-grain flours, milled complete with the cereal germ and bran and consequently still retaining the nutrients and the natural dietary fibre which are processed out of refined white products.

Black raisin loaf, Honey spice ring. Fennel rye bread, Walnut spongecake gâteau – all have a characteristic homeliness and a delicious nutty texture that more than compensates for the fact that, baked with the whole grain, they will never be light as a feather.

Bread, scones and teabreads, lowest in fat and sugar content, make sound nutritional sense for everyday baking. As our recipes show, you can ring the changes with herbs, spices and fruits (and increase the proportion of dried fruits to cut down still further on the sugar) until you and the family are spoiled for choice. Cutting down on sugars is essential to the spirit of wholefood cookery and it need be absolutely no hardship as you will find when you try our sugarless Celebration cake.

# FENNEL RYE BREAD

*Makes one 450 g (1 lb) loaf*

175 g (6 oz) strong wholewheat flour
175 g (6 oz) rye flour
½ teaspoon salt
1 teaspoon baking powder
40 g (1½ oz) soft margarine
150 ml (¼ pint) soured cream
1 egg
milk, for brushing
1 tablespoon fennel seeds

*Preparation time: 25 minutes*
*Cooking time: 1¼ hours*
*Oven: 200°C, 400°F, Gas Mark 6*

1. Sift together the flours, salt and baking powder and tip in any bran remaining in the sieve. Rub in the margarine. Beat together the soured cream and egg and stir into the dry ingredients to form a firm dough.
2. Knead the dough on a lightly-floured board until it is smooth. Shape it into a round and place it on a greased baking sheet. Brush the top of the loaf with milk and sprinkle on the fennel seeds.
3. Bake in a preheated oven for 1¼ hours, or until the bread sounds hollow when tapped. Transfer it to a wire rack to cool. **F** The bread is best eaten within 1 day of baking.

**F** *Freeze for up to 1 month. Thaw the baked loaf at room temperature for 6-7 hours.*

## SPICED PUMPKIN BREAD

*Makes one 900 g (2 lb) loaf*

450 g (1 lb) slice of pumpkin, peeled, seeded and chopped
450 g (1 lb) wholewheat flour
½ teaspoon salt
½ teaspoon ground ginger
½ teaspoon ground cinnamon
a pinch of grated nutmeg
1 sachet easy-blend dried yeast
150 ml (¼ pint) tepid milk
1 egg, beaten, to glaze
2 tablespoons blanched chopped almonds, for topping

*Preparation time: 1 hour, plus 1½ hours rising*
*Cooking time: 1½ hours*
*Oven: 200°C, 400°F, Gas Mark 6*

1. Steam the pumpkin over boiling water for 25-30 minutes, until it is soft. Press it through a sieve or liquidize it in a blender to make a purée. Set aside to cool slightly.
2. Sift the flour, salt, ginger, cinnamon and nutmeg and tip in any bran remaining in the sieve. Stir in the dried yeast. Beat in the pumpkin purée and milk and mix to a firm dough.
3. Knead the dough on a lightly-floured board until it is smooth and elastic – about 10 minutes if you are working by hand.
4. Place the dough in an oiled polythene bag and leave in a warm place for about 1 hour, or until it has doubled in size.
5. Knead the dough again for 5 minutes. Divide it into 2 pieces, one twice the size of the other. Press the greased handle of a wooden spoon down through the centre, to join the 2 pieces of dough together.
6. Place the dough on a baking sheet, cover and leave in a warm place to rise for 20-25 minutes.
7. Brush the top with beaten egg and scatter on the almonds.
8. Bake the loaf in a preheated oven for 55 minutes-1 hour, until it sounds hollow when tapped. Cool on a wire rack. F

F *Freeze for up to 1 month. Thaw for 6-7 hours at room temperature.*

*Clockwise from the left: Fennel rye bread; Spiced pumpkin bread; Banchory muffins.*

## BANCHORY MUFFINS

*Makes about 12 muffins*

100 g (4 oz) wholewheat self-raising flour
2 teaspoons baking powder
salt
75 g (3 oz) medium oatmeal
40 g (1½ oz) soft light brown sugar
75 g (3 oz) dried stoned dates, chopped
1 tablespoon set honey
15 g (½ oz) soft margarine
150 ml (¼ pint) buttermilk

*Preparation time: 20 minutes*
*Cooking time: 20 minutes*
*Oven: 200°C, 400°F, Gas Mark 6*

1. Mix together the flour, baking powder, salt, oatmeal, sugar and dates.
2. Melt the honey, margarine and buttermilk over a low heat, then cool slightly.
3. Pour the milk mixture on to the dry ingredients and stir quickly to form a smooth batter.
4. Spoon the mixture into deep patty tins, to come just over half-way up them.
5. Bake in a preheated oven for 15-18 minutes, until the muffins are well risen and firm.
6. Leave them to cool in the tins for 1-2 minutes, then remove the muffins from the tins and let them cool on a wire rack. F When they are completely cold, store them in an airtight tin.

F *Store the muffins in the freezer for up to 1 month. They can be thawed at room temperature for 1 hour.*

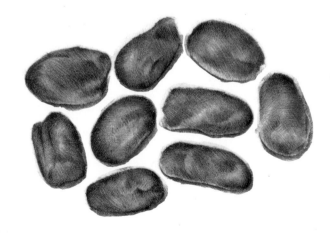

# BANANA AND YOGURT TEABREAD

*Makes 1 'barrel' loaf or
1 small loaf, just under 450 g (1 lb)*

50 g (2 oz) soft margarine
90 g (3½ oz) soft light brown sugar
1 egg, beaten
100 g (4 oz) wholewheat flour
salt
1 large banana, about 150 g (5 oz)
2 tablespoons plain unsweetened yogurt
50 g (2 oz) sultanas
2 tablespoons sunflower seeds

*Preparation time: 20 minutes
Cooking time: about 1¼ hours
Oven: 160°C, 325°F, Gas Mark 3*

1. Grease and flour a cleaned 825 g (29 oz) food can with the top removed or a 20 × 10 cm (8 × 4 inch) loaf tin.
2. Cream the margarine and sugar until they are light and fluffy, then beat in the egg.
3. Sift the flour and salt and tip in any bran left in the sieve. Mash the banana with the yogurt.
4. Add the flour mixture and the banana alternately to the creamed fat, beating well between each addition. Stir in the sultanas and sunflower seeds.
5. Spoon the mixture into the prepared can or loaf tin. Bake in a preheated oven for 1-1¼ hours, until the loaf is cooked. Test it by piercing the centre with a fine skewer.

# AYRSHIRE PAN SCONES

*Makes 12 wedges*

225 g (8 oz) strong wholewheat flour
1 teaspoon bicarbonate of soda
1 teaspoon salt
1 teaspoon cream of tartar
25 g (1 oz) soft margarine
15 g (½ oz) soft light brown sugar
150 ml (¼ pint) plain unsweetened yogurt
100 ml (3½ fl oz) soured cream
oil, for brushing

*Preparation time: 20 minutes
Cooking time: 30 minutes*

*Serve cut into wedges with honey and low fat soft cheese.*

1. Sift the flour, soda, salt and cream of tartar and tip in any bran remaining in the sieve. Rub in the margarine and stir in the sugar. Stir in the yogurt and soured cream. Shape the mixture into a dough and knead it lightly. **A**
2. Divide the dough into 2 equal pieces and shape each one to a round. Flatten the pieces until they are 2 cm (¾ inch) thick.
3. Heat a heavy-based frying pan and very lightly brush it with oil.

# HERB SCONES

*Makes about 8-10 scones*

225 g (8 oz) wholewheat flour
½ teaspoon bicarbonate of soda
½ teaspoon salt
40 g (1½ oz) white vegetable fat
1 teaspoon dried oregano
½ teaspoon dried basil
75 g (3 oz) Gouda cheese, grated
150 ml (¼ pint) buttermilk
1 tablespoon tomato purée
milk, for brushing

*Preparation time: 15 minutes*
*Cooking time: 20 minutes*
*Oven: 200°C, 400°F, Gas Mark 6*

*If you cannot obtain buttermilk – which, like yogurt, gives the necessary acid and the characteristic flavour to scones of all kinds, you can substitute milk soured with lemon juice. Stir in teaspoon lemon juice to each 300 ml ( pint) milk.*

1. Sift the flour, soda and salt and rub in the fat until the mixture is like fine breadcrumbs. Stir in the dried herbs and half the cheese. Gradually stir the milk into the tomato purée so that it is well blended. Pour the mixture on to the dry ingredients and mix to form a firm dough.
2. Roll out the dough on a lightly-floured board to a thickness of about 2 cm (¾ inch).
3. Using a 5 cm (2 inch) cutter, cut out rounds of the dough. Gather up the pieces into a ball, roll them out again and cut more rounds.
4. Place the scone rounds on a baking sheet and sprinkle them with the remaining cheese.
5. Bake in a preheated oven for 20 minutes, or until the scones are well risen and springy to the touch.
6. Transfer them to a wire rack to cool.

4. Cook each scone over moderate heat for 6-7 minutes, until it is well browned on the underside. Flip it over and cook the other side. Transfer the scone to a wire rack to cool. Cook the remaining dough in the same way. [F]

[A] *These scones do not stay fresh for more than 1 day, but the dough can be made in advance, wrapped in foil and stored in the refrigerator overnight. Leave it to relax at room temperature for about 30 minutes before cooking.*

[F] *Freeze for up to 1 month. Thaw the scones in the oven at 180°C, 350°F, Gas Mark 4 for 10-15 minutes.*

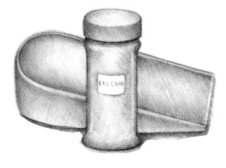

*Clockwise from the top: Banana and yogurt teabread; Herb scones; Ayrshire pan scones.*

# BLACK RAISIN LOAF

*Makes one 900 g (2 lb) loaf*

350 g (12 oz) wholewheat flour
1 tablespoon baking powder
1 teaspoon salt
1 teaspoon mixed ground spice
a large pinch of grated nutmeg
100 g (4 oz) medium oatmeal
150 g (5 oz) soft margarine
150 g (5 oz) soft light brown sugar
2 eggs, beaten
175 g (6 oz) seedless raisins
50 g (2 oz) dried stoned dates, chopped
150 ml (¼ pint) milk
7 tablespoons molasses, melted

*Preparation time: 20 minutes*
*Cooking time: about 2 hours*
*Oven: 180°C, 350°F, Gas Mark 4*

*1.* Grease and line a loose-bottomed 23 cm (9 inch) round tin with greased greaseproof paper.

*2.* Sift together the flour, baking powder, salt and spices. Tip in any bran remaining in the sieve and stir in the oatmeal.

*3.* Cream together the margarine and sugar until the mixture is light and fluffy. Beat in the eggs and dry ingredients alternately. Stir in the raisins and dates and beat in the milk and molasses. Beat well until the mixture is quite smooth.

*4.* Turn the mixture into the prepared tin. Bake in a preheated oven for 1¾-2 hours, or until the loaf is cooked. To test, pierce the centre with a dry skewer. It should come out clean, with no trace of moisture.

*5.* Stand the tin on a wire rack to cool. **F**

**F** *When cold peel off the greaseproof paper and close-wrap the loaf in foil. Freeze for up to 3 months. To thaw it leave it at room temperature for 6-7 hours.*

*From the left: Black raisin loaf; Sesame bagels.*

# SESAME BAGELS

*Makes 16 rings*

450 g (1 lb) wholewheat flour
5 tablespoons sesame seeds
1 teaspoon salt
1 teaspoon soft light brown sugar
15 g (½ oz) 'instant' dried yeast
150 ml (¼ pint) milk
5 tablespoons hot water
1 tablespoon sunflower oil
1 egg, beaten

*Preparation time: 1 hour, plus 2 hours rising*
*Cooking time: 35 minutes*
*Oven: 220°C, 425°F, Gas Mark 7*

*Serve Sesame Bagels hot, as a snack, or to accompany a light meal of soup or salad.*

1. Mix the flour, 3 tablespoons of the sesame seeds, the salt, sugar and yeast. Mix together the milk, water, oil and egg, and pour on to the dry ingredients. Beat to form a firm dough.

2. Knead the dough thoroughly on a lightly-floured board until it is elastic – this takes about 10 minutes by hand.

3. Place the dough in an oiled polythene bag and leave it in a warm place for about 1½ hours, or until it has doubled in size.

4. Knead the dough again for about 3 minutes – this is known as 'knocking back'.

5. Cut the dough into 16 pieces and roll them into balls. Use the oiled handle of a wooden spoon to push a hole through the centre of each one.

6. Place the rings on a greased baking sheet. Leave in a warm place to rise again for 20 minutes.

7. Bring a large pan of water to the boil and poach the bagels in batches for 30-45 seconds, until they expand. Lift them out with a draining spoon and dry them on crumpled pieces of kitchen paper.

8. Bake the bagels in a preheated oven for 30 minutes, until they are well risen. Toss the bagels at once in the remaining sesame seeds. Serve hot.

# WHEATGERM BREAD

*Makes two 450 g (1 lb) loaves*

450 g (1 lb) strong wholewheat flour
50 g (2 oz) bran
75 g (3 oz) wheatgerm
1 tablespoon soft light brown sugar
15 g (½ oz) 'instant' dried yeast
2 teaspoons salt
300 ml (½ pint) tepid water
1 tablespoon sunflower oil
2 tablespoons caraway seeds, for topping

*Preparation time: 25 minutes, plus 2 hours rising*
*Cooking time: 35 minutes*
*Oven: 230°C, 450°F, Gas Mark 8;*
*then: 200°C, 400°F, Gas Mark 6*

1. Grease two 450 g (1 lb) loaf tins.
2. Mix together the flour, bran, wheatgerm, sugar, yeast and salt. Pour on the water and oil and mix to a firm dough.
3. Knead the dough on a lightly-floured board for 10 minutes, or until it is smooth.
4. Place the dough in an oiled polythene bag and leave it to rise in a warm place for 1-1¼ hours, until it has doubled in size.
5. Knead the dough again for 5 minutes. Divide it into pieces of equal size.
6. Press the dough into the prepared loaf tins and level the tops. Sprinkle on the caraway seed topping.
7. Cover the tins and leave them in a warm place to rise for 30-40 minutes, until the dough is level with the top of the tin.
8. Bake the loaves in a preheated oven for 5 minutes. Reduce the heat and bake for 30 minutes more. The loaves should sound hollow when tapped.
9. Stand the loaves in their tins on a wire rack to cool. F

F *Thaw the loaves at room temperature for 5-6 hours.*

*From the left: Wheatgerm bread; Walnut spongecake gâteau.*

# WALNUT SPONGECAKE GÂTEAU

*Makes one 19 cm (7½ inch) cake*

175 g (6 oz) self-raising 81% wheatmeal flour
1 teaspoon baking powder
175 g (6 oz) soft margarine
175 g (6 oz) soft light brown sugar
75 g (3 oz) walnuts, finely chopped
2 teaspoons lemon rind
3 eggs
1 tablespoon lemon juice
*Filling and topping:*
350 g (12 oz) low fat soft cheese
about 3 tablespoons clear honey
3 peaches, stoned, skinned and thinly sliced
1 tablespoon lemon juice

*Preparation time: 30 minutes*
*Cooking time: 40 minutes*
*Oven: 180°C, 350°F, Gas Mark 4*

1. Grease two 19 cm (7½ inch) sandwich tins.
2. Sift the flour and baking powder and tip in any bran left in the sieve. Add the margarine, sugar, walnuts, lemon rind and eggs and beat well until the mixture is smooth. Beat in the lemon juice.
3. Divide the mixture between the sandwich tins. Level the tops, then make a very slight dip in the centre of each.
4. Bake in a preheated oven for 35-40 minutes, until the cakes are firm but springy to the touch.
5. Stand the tins on a wire rack to cool. Turn out the cakes and leave them to become completely cold. **F**
6. Beat the cheese and honey and add a little more honey if the mixture still tastes salty. Toss the peach slices in the lemon juice as soon as they are cut.
7. Spread half the cheese on to one half of the cake as a filling, and arrange most of the peach slices on top. Spread the remaining cheese on top of the second layer. Sandwich the 2 layers together and decorate the top with the reserved peach slices.

**F** *Freeze the 2 sponge sandwich layers separately, close-wrapped in foil. Thaw at room temperature for 4 hours.*

## APRICOT CAKE

*Makes one 18 cm (7 inch) cake*

100 g (4 oz) soft margarine
100 g (4 oz) soft light brown sugar
2 large eggs, beaten
200 g (7 oz) wholewheat self-raising flour
½ teaspoon baking powder
½ teaspoon ground cinnamon
225 g (8 oz) dried apricots, soaked, drained and
chopped
100 g (4 oz) seedless raisins
2 tablespoons demerara sugar
*Topping:*
100 g (4 oz) dried apricots, soaked and drained
150 ml (¼ pint) soured cream
1 tablespoon clear honey
2 tablespoons blanched almonds, toasted and
chopped

*Preparation time: 35 minutes*
*Cooking time: 2½ hours*
*Oven: 160°C, 325°F, Gas Mark 3*

*1.* Grease and line an 18 cm (7 inch) cake tin.
*2.* Beat the margarine and sugar together until it
is light and fluffy, then gradually beat in the
eggs. Sift the flour, baking powder and cinnamon and tip in any bran left in the sieve. Add
the dry ingredients, a little at a time to the
creamed mixture. Stir in the apricots and
raisins and beat well.
*3.* Turn the mixture into the prepared cake tin,
level the top and sprinkle on the demerara
sugar.
*4.* Bake in a pre-heated oven for 1½ hours, or
until a skewer pierced through the centre of the
cake comes out clean.
*5.* Stand the cake in its tin on a wire rack to cool.
Then peel off the paper and leave the cake to
become completely cool. **F**
*6.* Liquidize the apricots in a blender and beat in
the soured cream and honey.
*7.* Spread the topping over the cake. Sprinkle the
chopped nuts around the edge, to decorate.

**F** *Open-freeze the cake, then close-wrap it in foil and freeze
for up to 6 months. Thaw at room temperature for 6-7 hours.*

## CAROB HONEY CAKE

*Makes one 20 cm (8 inch) flat cake*

75 g (3 oz) soft light brown sugar
175 g (6 oz) clear honey
50 g (2 oz) wholewheat flour
3 tablespoons carob powder
½ teaspoon ground cinnamon
25 g (1 oz) ground almonds
1 tablespoon orange rind
50 g (2 oz) candied orange peel, chopped
175 g (6 oz) hazelnuts
100 g (4 oz) blanched almonds, lightly toasted

*Preparation time: 20 minutes*
*Cooking time: 40 minutes*
*Oven: 140°C, 275°F, Gas Mark 1*

*To store the cake, close-wrap it in foil once it is cold and put it in a container in the refrigerator. If the cake is left for very long at room temperature it soon becomes sticky.*

1. Melt the sugar and honey over a low heat, then bring to simmering point and simmer, stirring frequently, for 10 minutes.
2. Sift the flour, carob powder and cinnamon, tip in any bran left in the sieve and stir in the ground almonds and orange rind. Pour on the honey mixture, stir quickly then stir in the peel and nuts. Beat thoroughly.
3. Spread the mixture into a 20 cm (8 inch) greased and floured plain flan ring on a baking sheet or a loose-based tin.
4. Bake in a preheated oven for 30 minutes, until the cake is firm.
5. Cool the cake in the flan ring on a wire rack.

# SPICY CARROT CAKE

*Makes one 23 cm (9 inch) cake*

2 medium bananas, mashed
150 g (5 oz) soft light brown sugar
3 eggs, beaten
275 g (10 oz) wholewheat flour
1 teaspoon bicarbonate of soda
1 teaspoon salt
2 teaspoons baking powder
1 teaspoon mixed ground spice
50 g (2 oz) walnuts, chopped
175 ml (6 fl oz) sunflower oil
175 g (6 oz) carrot, grated
*Topping:*
175 g (6 oz) low fat soft cheese
40 g (1½ oz) soft light brown sugar
1 teaspoon lemon rind
2 teaspoons lemon juice
lemon slices, quartered to decorate

*Preparation time: 30 minutes*
*Cooking time: 1 hour 5 minutes*
*Oven: 180°C, 350°F, Gas Mark 4*

1. Grease and line a 23 cm (9 inch) round cake tin.
2. Beat the bananas and sugar until they are well blended. Gradually beat in the eggs. Sift the flour, soda, salt, baking powder and spice and beat into the banana mixture a little at a time with the chopped walnuts. Beat in the oil, then stir in the grated carrot. Beat well until the mixture is smooth.
3. Turn the mixture into the prepared cake tin.
4. Bake in a preheated oven for about 1 hour 5 minutes, or until the cake is 'set' and golden brown. Test by piercing it through the centre with a fine skewer, which should come out clean if the cake is done.
5. Leave the cake in the tin and place on a wire rack to cool. Then peel off the paper and leave the cake to become completely cold.
6. Mix together in a bowl the cheese, sugar, lemon rind and juice.
7. Spread the mixture over the top of the cake. Arrange the lemon slices on top to decorate.

*Clockwise from the top: Carrot cake; Carob honey cake; Apricot cake*

# CELEBRATION CAKE

*Makes one 20 cm (8 inch) cake*

200 g (7 oz) dried stoned dates, finely chopped
150 ml (¼ pint) milk, plus extra if needed (see
method)
100 g (4 oz) soft margarine
3 eggs, beaten
225 g (8 oz) wholewheat flour
2 teaspoons baking powder
1 teaspoon ground cinnamon
½ teaspoon ground ginger
a large pinch of grated nutmeg
2 teaspoons orange rind
1 tablespoon orange juice
50 g (2 oz) ground almonds
50 g (2 oz) blanched almonds, chopped
225 g (8 oz) seedless raisins
175 g (6 oz) currants
50 g (2 oz) sultanas
50 g (2 oz) candied orange peel, chopped
*Apricot paste:*
100 g (4 oz) blanched almonds
225 g (8 oz) dried apricots, chopped
2 tablespoons soft light brown sugar
1 tablespoon lemon juice
1 tablespoon clear honey, warmed

*Preparation time: 1 hour*
*Cooking time: 3¼ hours*
*Oven: 150°C, 300°F, Gas Mark 2*

1. Grease a 20 cm (8 inch) cake tin and line it with greased greaseproof paper.
2. Mash the dates with the milk and heat them over a very low heat, stirring constantly, until they form a thick paste. Set aside to cool.
3. Beat the cooled date paste with the margarine. Beat in the eggs, a little at a time.
4. Sift the flour, baking powder and spices. Add any bran left in the sieve and the orange rind.
5. Gradually add the dry ingredients to the date mixture, beating all the time. Beat in the orange juice, ground and chopped almonds, raisins, currants, sultanas and peel. Beat the mixture well and add a very little milk if necessary to give a firm dropping consistency.
6. Turn the mixture into the prepared tin and level the top.
7. Bake in a preheated oven for 2¾-3 hours, until a fine skewer pierced through the centre of the cake comes out clean.
8. Leave the cake in the tin and stand it on a wire rack to cool. **F**

9. To make the apricot paste, grind the almonds until they are as fine as semolina. Reserve 2 teaspoons of the ground almonds, then add the apricots, sugar and lemon juice and process to a smooth paste. Knead the paste on a board lightly sprinkled with the remaining ground almonds. **A**
10. Roll out the paste to a thickness of 5 mm (¼ inch) and cut out decorative shapes, and a thick band to cover the side of the cake. Brush

the side of the cake with the honey and press on the strip of apricot paste. Ⓐ Ⓕ Brush the decoration for the top with honey and press on to the top of the cake. Close-wrap the cake in foil and store it in an airtight tin.

Ⓐ *You can make the apricot paste in advance, wrap it in foil and store it in an airtight container. You can also store the cut-out shapes, stacked between layers of greaseproof paper or polythene.*
Ⓕ *Prewrap the cake when cold and freeze for up to 3 months. Thaw at room temperature.*

# HONEY SPICE RING

*Makes one 1 litre (1¾ pint) ring cake*

150 g (5 oz) soft margarine
50 g (2 oz) soft light brown sugar
3 tablespoons clear honey
2 eggs, beaten
175 g (6 oz) wholewheat self-raising flour
1½ teaspoons mixed ground spice
½ teaspoon ground ginger
75 g (3 oz) walnuts, chopped
*Filling:*
225 g (8 oz) cottage cheese, sieved
150 ml (¼ pint) plain unsweetened yogurt
50 g (2 oz) soft light brown sugar
50 g (2 oz) candied orange peel, chopped
50 g (2 oz) seedless raisins
25 g (1 oz) blanched almonds, chopped
1 tablespoon orange rind

*Preparation time: overnight draining, then 1 hour*
*Cooking time: 40 minutes*
*Oven: 180°C, 350°F, Gas Mark 4*

*1.* Grease and flour a 1 litre (1¾ pint) ring mould.
*2.* Prepare the filling the day before. Beat the cheese, yogurt and sugar. Stir in the peel, raisins, almonds and orange rind and beat well.
*3.* Line a sieve with a double layer of scalded muslin. Spoon in the cheese filling, cover it with muslin and put a plate and heavy weight on top. Leave the cheese to drain overnight.
*4.* Cream the margarine, sugar and honey until the mixture is light and fluffy. Stir in the eggs. Sift the flour and spices and tip in any bran left in the sieve. Fold the flour into the creamed mixture and stir in the walnuts.
*5.* Spoon the mixture into the prepared mould.
*6.* Stand the mould on a baking tray and bake in a preheated oven for 40 minutes, until the cake is well risen.
*7.* Leave the cake to cool in the mould, then turn it out on to a wire rack until completely cold.
*8.* Turn the cake on to a serving dish. Fork over the cheese filling and spoon some into the centre of the ring.

**Variation:** *The cheese filling is a simple adaptation of the Russian Easter dessert known as pashka. It is also delicious served with fresh or simmered soft fruits.*

*From the top: Celebration cake; Honey spice ring (variation).*

**ACKNOWLEDGMENTS**
The publishers would like to thank the following
who were involved in the preparation of this book:
Photographer James Jackson with stylist Sue
Russell
Food prepared for photography by Allyson Birch
Illustrations by Jane Brewster

The publishers would also like to thank the
following companies for their kindness in
providing equipment used in the photography for
this book:
David Mellor, 4 Sloane Square, London SW1
Elizabeth David, 46 Bourne Street, London SW1